QUALITY AND EQUALITY
Promoting opportunities in schools

Kathryn A. Riley

CASSELL

To my daughter Jo
And in memory of my mother Agnes

Cassell
Villiers House   387 Park Avenue South
41/47 Strand   New York
London WC2N 5JE   NY 10016-8810

© Kathryn A. Riley 1994

First published 1994

British Library Cataloguing-in-Publication Data
A catalogue record for this book is available from the British Library.

ISBN 0-304-32687-9 (hardback)
     0-304-32688-7 (paperback)

Typeset by Litho Link Ltd, Welshpool, Powys, Wales
Printed and bound in Great Britain

EDUCATION MANAGEMENT SERIES
Series editor: John Sayer

QUALITY AND EQUALITY

TITLES IN THE EDUCATION MANAGEMENT SERIES

M. Bottery:
The Ethics of Educational Management: Personal, Social and Political Perspectives on School Organization

M. Hattersley (ed.):
The Appraisal of Headteachers

I. Lawrence:
Power and Politics at the Department of Education and Science

P. Leighton:
Schools and Employment Law

J. Sayer:
The Future Governance of Education

Contents

Foreword by the series editor   vii

Acknowledgements   viii

Introduction   ix

Part I   The Context

1 Quality and equality: competing or complementary objectives?   3

2 Education: the shift from egalitarianism to competition   17

Part II   The Educational Experience

3 The educational experience   35

4 Black and white girls – yesterday and today   57

Part III   Prescription for Action

5 Leadership   87

6 Quality and equality: evaluating the context and the outcomes   105

7 Quality and equality – and the pursuit of common objectives   127

Bibliography   135

Name index   145

Subject index   147

History . . . the quarrels of popes and kings, with wars or pestilences, in every page; the men all so good for nothing, and hardly any women at all – it is very tiresome . . .

Jane Austen, *Northanger Abbey*

Foreword by the series editor

This book has an important place in a series intended to address major issues in ways which will inform reflected practice in managing schools and services. It is written from a background of wide experience and careful investigation, by an author who brings together principles and practice. Other books in the series, notably those by Mike Bottery and Pat Leighton, raise important management questions about equal opportunities. These questions are explored here with a depth and thoroughness which will make this a key reference point and inspiration in the next decade.

Management in education demands a balance between educational and professional issues, between learning and enabling organization, and these are usefully interwoven in Kathryn Riley's proposals for action. The book exposes the mythical polarity between quality and equality and shows these to be essential to each other. It points to development needed in both women and men if education services are to become fully human. For the education service as a whole and for any part of it, a shared commitment to quality in creating access and providing opportunities for all is needed in statements and actions.

This is a most valuable text from which to analyse and evaluate current trends and to re-examine policy and practice at all levels. Equity and excellence in education are indivisible.

John Sayer

Acknowledgements

I am indebted to all the young women I have interviewed over the last decade and to the co-operation of their teachers. Many people have contributed to my thinking about the issues covered in this book, including Mary Fuller and Gerald Grace (my PhD supervisors of many years ago), and, more recently, colleagues at INLOGOV, in particular Chris Skelcher, Kieron Walsh and Judy White. I would also like to thank Dot Woolley for her help, Maggie Sandra and Bernard Riley for their constant encouragement and John Tilley for his unfailing support.

Introduction

The radical reforms of the British education system in the 1980s can be typified as a concentration on the search for 'Quality'. This focus has replaced, often to the extent of conscious rejection of, the emphasis of the previous decades on 'Equality' – equality first of class and then of gender and race.

The two approaches have been widely regarded as entrenched opposites, as alternatives that must battle for superiority. They have been fitted into the conventional antagonistic framework: liberal versus marketeers; Labour versus Conservative; collectivist versus individualist.

This book suggests that there are many more points of similarity and of compatibility between the two approaches than the partisans on both sides will admit.

It would be ridiculous to suggest that there is no difference between the educational landscapes of the 1960s, 1970s and 1980s, or the policy and political priorities. Whilst the book does not attempt to synthesize all the various educational theories which have vied for attention and support over the past 30 years, it does seek to explore an assorted range of specific areas and topics which throw a new light on the Quality and Equality debate, particularly in the context of the most recent education changes. It tentatively suggests that there are some common threads: some points at which the ends of one approach can be achieved by the means of the other.

It has suited many people to cherish a polarized view of educational thinking: to see a gaping chasm yawning between two cliffs marked Quality and Equality. This book throws a few lines across the gulf and suggests that it may be neither as wide or as deep as it is often represented.

In making this exploration, gender has been the major focus. But issues of gender cannot be separated from other areas of structural inequality, such as race and class, sex, disablement and age, which are also integral to the experience of girls and women using and providing the education service.

The book addresses issues of both policy and practice. It draws on the author's experience as a teacher, researcher, local government officer, school governor and parent, in an attempt to provide a bridge between theory, policy-making and practice. It offers a framework for action on quality and equality.

There are three parts. Part I (Chapters 1 and 2) examines the national context for the debate on quality. Chapter 1 traces its origins and its implications for education services, arguing that the pursuit of equality is an essential component of quality and that the exercise of discretion is a key component of action. Chapter 2 explores the impact of recent education legislation on the powers and responsibilities of local authorities, schools and governors and the implications for quality and equality.

Part II (Chapters 3 and 4) focuses on the processes and outcomes of schooling for girls over the past century and approaches to the education of black and ethnic minority children over the past 20 years. It argues that despite the improvement in girls' examination performance, women and girls are still being disadvantaged by their schooling and face discrimination in the labour market. Gender still needs to be a focus for policy-makers, researchers and practitioners.

Within this second part of the book, Chapter 4 draws on some original research carried out by the author in the early 1980s on race and gender in secondary schools, and contrasts the educational experience of the young black and white women in that research with that of their 1990s counterparts.

Part III (Chapters 5, 6 and 7) provides an agenda for review, action and change, exploring how quality and equality issues can be drawn together. Chapter 5 bridges description and prescription with an analysis of women's unequal access to positions of educational leadership and a suggestion that women leaders and managers have much to contribute to the development of a high-quality educational service. It also focuses on educational leadership, exploring the effectiveness of different leadership styles, their possible connection with gender and how any such relationship would impact on the debate about quality and equality.

Chapter 6 examines contemporary issues of performance and evaluation, identifying strategies to build an education indicators database which would integrate dimensions of quality and equality.

Finally, Chapter 7 examines the scope which all the prime movers in the education service (national and local government officials, governors, funding agencies, schools, colleges, teachers and the consumers of the service) have to exercise their discretion to pursue quality and equality objectives.

PART I

THE CONTEXT

Chapter 1

Quality and equality: competing or complementary objectives?

Quality and equality are interconnected: not separate entities but inseparable features of any good education provision. Fostering quality and equality requires an awareness of the obstacles which individuals face in achieving their potential and of the barriers which obstruct harmonious relationships between groups and individuals. Resolving such equality issues is a route to quality.

The equality issue facing pupils and teachers also needs to be viewed together. The differential educational experience offered to girls and boys, black and white pupils is connected to that offered to teachers – female and male, black and white. Equality in the classroom cannot be separated from equality in the staffroom. It is a shared agenda – a shared experience.

In seeking to develop a strategy which incorporates both quality and equality, tensions and dilemmas are bound to arise for providers and receivers of the education services because decisions about the nature of services, who receives them and how they are delivered are not neutral. They depend on value judgements made by those involved in education: teachers, governors, administrators and policy-makers. Each of these groups has varying degrees of discretion to influence educational processes and outcomes. Decisions that they make – or fail to make – will impact differentially on students and staff. This chapter explores the context of the debate on quality and equality and the scope which the key groups have to influence both educational processes and outcomes.

THE QUEST FOR QUALITY

Over the past decade quality has been the buzzword: *quality services*, a *quality educational experience*, total *quality management*. Quality has entered into the vocabulary of the educational professionals, politicians and the myriad individuals, groups and organizations that claim a stake in the education service.

But although quality in education has apparently become a national goal, definitions are elusive, or maybe illusory. A major OECD report on schools and quality has argued against providing one simple definition of quality in education and has suggested instead that we need a clearer understanding of how context – curriculum, school organization, resources and facilities, and evaluation of pupils, teachers and systems – can contribute to quality (OECD, 1989). As with any value-laden concept, definitions of quality change over time and vary for different individuals and groups. Attempts to improve quality raise questions about the aims of society, the purposes of schooling and the nature of participation.

Much current thinking about the concept of quality has originated in the manufacturing sector. Concerns about manufacturing quality and standards stem from the late nineteenth- and early twentieth-century decline in skilled workers and the consequent difficulties caused for mass production. Quality control was introduced in the 1920s in an attempt to increase the percentage of sound products manufactured. After World War II there was a shift in emphasis from quality control to quality assurance, an activity which focused on the pre-production planning in an attempt to develop processes and procedures that would minimize faulty production.

The 'quality revolution' took place in Japan in the 1950s assisted by seminal figures such as Deming and Duran (Macdonald and Piggott, 1990). Deming emphasized quality assurance and the importance of creating a quality culture. He argued that until the 1950s definitions of quality in manufacturing had tended to rest on what the experts thought customers wanted, rather than on information about what customers actually wanted.

The rise of consumerism, particularly in the USA, shifted attention to the customer voice. Quality became everyone's business. Customers would make decisions about quality, insomuch as they could exercise choice by withholding their purchasing power. This approach has been sustained through the 1980s and into the 1990s by theorists such as Peters and Waterman (1982), who have argued that being 'closer to the customer' is a fundamental attribute of a successful company.

QUALITY IN THE PUBLIC AND PRIVATE SECTORS

Manufacturing and other private sector notions of quality began to permeate the public sector in the UK at the national level with the election of the 1979 Conservative government, and over the last decade they have been linked to the development of measures to assess performance of public sector organizations. Many local authorities have responded to the quality drive by developing a new focus on services and customers and by finding new ways to evaluate the quality and impact of their services.

There are difficulties, however, in transferring private sector models about quality into the public sector. To begin with, the common language increasingly used in both the public and private sector masks some fundamental differences. The term 'customer', for example, is used today for shoppers as well as for users of services such as education.

But the education 'customer' hardly resembles the supermarket shopper. The purchasing power of the education consumer is limited. Only a minority have the financial power to exit from the public education service. And exercising this power will not pressurize the management to improve the service; indeed, if those who can afford to exit the service do so, the pressure for public sector resources for education falls, having lost the involvement of the wealthiest, most powerful and articulate parents. All parents as 'customers' of the education service supposedly have the right to choose a school, but not necessarily the possibility of exercising that choice. Indeed, there is increasing evidence to suggest that it is schools that are choosing parents and children. Furthermore, the education customer *has* to buy; the supermarket customer can just walk out of the shop without purchasing.

The education service has become imbued with the language and concepts of quality. Many local education authorities have striven to develop the mechanisms and processes of inspection as one essential way of validating quality and of giving certain key stakeholders in education (headteachers and governors) a handle.

> The fundamental principle is that headteachers and governors must have a view about quality. The inspectors' role is to authenticate that view. It is essential that schools have an objective evaluation of quality . . . For these you need procedures and competency.
>
> (Riley, 1992a, p. 14)

Other local education authorities have set up quality assurance teams, or have described their activities in marketing or business terms: 'quality control', 'managing a franchise'.

> Quality control becomes about process – what actually happens, it should not be about identifying failings but about showing that improvement is possible for all. This is the *raison d'être* of the process view of school improvement.
>
> The LEA is managing a franchise. Schools market that franchise. Each school has its own character but it shares communal objectives which make it part of the club. The underpinning element for all schools is to make them healthy and buoyant . . . If local education authorities think towards that end, it will provide them with a framework.
>
> (Ibid., pp. 17–18)

Chapter 2 will suggest, however, that in the light of recent legislation, local authorities will have to develop very different approaches to quality. Essential to any new framework will be the need to integrate equality issues – the wider lessons from equalities work have rarely been incorporated into broader quality goals – and to have clarity about the differences between quality in the public and private sectors.

Skelcher (1992) has argued that the differences between the way that the public and commercial sectors approach quality spring from their structural characteristics. There are differences in *accountability* (local authorities have a wider and more public range of accountability structures than the private sector); *choice* (local authorities work to enable local citizens to exercise choice: choice in commercial enterprises is linked to market concerns); and *purpose* (local authorities have a range of purposes: the provision of services, regulation, facilitation of local needs: commercial purposes are not exclusively but are largely geared to profit). All of these differences, summarized in Table 1.1, govern the way the two kinds of enterprise deal with their customers.

Despite these differences, commercial and public sector are united in needing to get it right for both customers and staff. Skelcher argues, however, that local authorities have not been sufficiently customer-orientated in the past, nor had a clear enough

Table 1.1 Comparison of local government and commercial sectors

	Local government	Commercial
Accountability	Extensive Open	Limited Closed
Choice	Wide value base Political process Customer also citizen	Narrow value base Managerial process Limited influence customer
Purpose	Multiple	Narrow

Source: Skelcher (1992)

focus on quality. A strategy for quality requires a clearer information base about service usage; improved access to services; the development of performance indicators which are customer-based; and changes in organizational culture so that professional differences do not create barriers to service provision.

Customer care initiatives (identifying who the customers are and what they want, and examining the impact of services on particular groups) have been one way in which local authorities have tried to focus more clearly on quality. Improving quality requires authorities to recognize the needs, background and experiences of individuals and also to recognize that services are of value only if they are judged to be of value by recipients (LGMB, 1991; LGIU, 1991a).

CREATING A BRIDGE BETWEEN QUALITY AND EQUALITY

But quality strategies can succeed in meeting the needs of customers only if they take into account the diverse views and perspectives of a range of groups. Quality is not a universal concept: what represents quality for one user may not do so for another.

> Quality cannot be defined separately from use and user experience. This means that a service that provides quality for one user may not provide quality for another, because needs, requirements and expectations may vary. Specifying service quality will always involve considering how users experience and evaluate a service and understanding the circumstances in which they will use it.
>
> (Stewart and Walsh, 1990, p. 4)

In assessing the impact of services on particular groups, customer care initiatives have begun to grapple with the links between quality and equality. Stewart and Walsh have suggested that three essential elements contribute to a framework for quality:

- whether the core service fits the purpose for which it was designed;
- the physical surroundings in which the service is delivered;
- and the service relationship between those who provide and those who receive the service.

This framework is a useful one for examining the inter-relationship between quality and equality. The core services question, 'Does the service meet the requirements of those for whom it is provided?', cannot be answered without knowing who the customers are: their gender, ethnic background and age. Similarly, the physical and social conditions of provision have to be viewed in the context of whether the services are physically accessible and whether customers, or clients, are encouraged or discouraged from taking up the service. Finally, the quality of the service relationship depends on whether those who are delivering the service understand the needs of those who are receiving the service. The questions posed in Figure 1.1 apply not only to local authorities but also to schools and institutions.

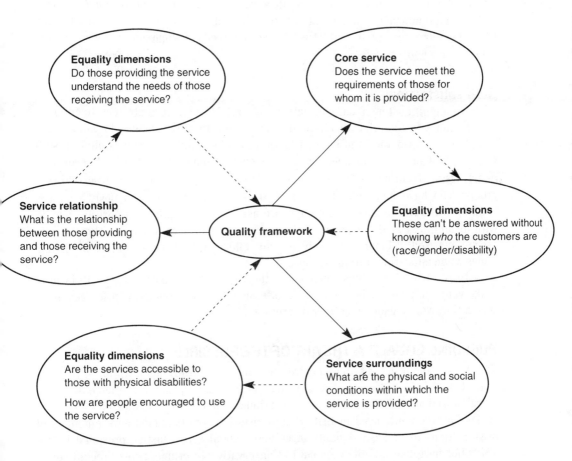

Figure 1.1   *Quality and equality: an inter-related network*

7

The integration of equality issues within quality initiatives is, however, problematic. Tensions and dilemmas can be created by competing priorities about consumer satisfaction, effective use of resources and staff satisfaction.

Consumer satisfaction

Evaluation of whether consumer satisfaction has been achieved highlights the tension between judging quality in terms of general levels of satisfaction and looking at quality from the perspective of disadvantaged groups. Satisfaction levels may vary between those who have experienced targeted improvement and other groups.

Effective use of resources

The objective of achieving the most effective use of resources has to be viewed within the context of diminishing resources for local authorities, colleges and schools. In striving for 'value for money' there is a tension between devoting resources to activities which will benefit the community at large and devoting resources to those which will provide most benefit to disadvantaged groups. For example, a 'One O'Clock' club may act as a general but time-limited amenity for parents in a locality but a day nursery will more effectively serve the needs of single parents who need to seek employment.

Staff satisfaction

In introducing customer care initiatives as part of their core strategy to improve quality, many local authorities have also developed training packages for staff aimed at enhancing autonomy and job satisfaction. But local authorities have limited staff training budgets and will need to make decisions about the balance of resources: general staff training as against targeted training opportunities for disadvantaged groups who have had limited access to training. An emphasis on positive action training will advantage certain groups (women, black and ethnic minorities, people with disabilities) at the expense of the dominant group (white men). (These issues are summarized in Figure 1.2.) Schools and colleges will also have to look at similar issues when allocating training resources.

In resolving these tensions, local authorities, schools and colleges will have to make value judgements based on their assessments about competing priorities. In so doing, they will be exercising their discretion.

PURSUING EQUALITY: THE ART OF THE POSSIBLE

The debate about equality has received less national government attention recently than the debate about quality and has often been disparate, fragmented and marginalized at a local level. Resource maximization and social justice have been the two main arguments used in Britain, and elsewhere, to persuade governments and organizations to tackle inequality. Arguments about social justice prevailed in the 1970s but have had a limited appeal to Conservative governments over recent years. Arguments about resource maximization have found greater support but have been

Objective	Quality	Equality
Consumer satisfaction	General level of consumer satisfaction	Activities may be focused on needs of specific groups
	Quality for one group of users may not be the same for all users	
Effective use of resources	Emphasis on 'value for money' for community at large	Emphasis on disadvantaged groups
	Limited resources may mean services need to be targeted to those in greatest need	
Staff satisfaction	Emphasis on 'customer care' can enhance staff autonomy and job satisfaction overall	Activities aimed at redressing past inequalities
	Emphasis on positive action training may appear to advantage certain groups at expense of dominant group (white men)	

Figure 1.2 *Quality and equality: tensions and dilemmas*

dependent on labour market trends.[1] Equality has not featured as a major government objective in the education revolution being wrought by central government. Whilst the achievement of quality objectives has become a mandatory feature of life in education, the achievement of equality has remained largely in the realms of discretion.

It is axiomatic that quality in education is a goal of governments. The pursuit of quality is the *raison d'être* of government: a basis of their mandate. The pursuit of equality, however, is a much more discretionary activity reflecting both the values of national government and the purposes of other policy-makers and practitioners in the system. Given that interpretations of quality are value-laden, it is therefore unsurprising that national governments have varied significantly in the extent to which they supported equality as a national goal. According to an OECD Report on school effectiveness, many governments have pursued a minimalist line on equal opportunities whilst others, such as those of Sweden and Norway, have pursued strong interventionist policies, predicated on a fundamental national commitment to equality goals (Chapman, 1991).

In the UK the settings for equality policies have been set down in legislation through:

the Disabled Persons Employment Act 1944, which requires organizations of more than 20 people to employ at least 3 per cent registered disabled people (unless they gain an exemption from this duty);

the Sex Discrimination Act 1975 and the Race Relations Act 1976, which cover direct and indirect discrimination in employment and services: the latter also places a duty on local authorities to promote equality of opportunity;

9

and through the Equal Pay Act 1983, which requires women and men who carry out the same type of work, or work of equal value, to be paid the same.

But British governments over the last decade have rarely intervened to pursue equality objectives. One notable exception has been in Northern Ireland, where the government has used the strongly interventionist policy of contract compliance to influence employment practices in respect of religious affiliation. The British government also reluctantly agreed to incorporate the concept of equal pay for work of equal value into UK legislation (through the 1983 Equal Pay Act) in response to the jurisdiction of the European courts. In general terms, however, the pursuit of equality objectives in the UK has largely been exercised through the discretionary activities of individuals and organizations.

Discretion is therefore a concept which needs some exploration. It can be defined in a number of ways: narrowly, as how key actors, in exceptional cases, depart from rules that they are expected to follow (Bull, 1980, quoted in Lidstrom, 1991), or, more broadly, as how 'a public officer has discretion within the effective limits of "his" powers to make a choice amongst possible courses of action, or inaction' (Davis, 1969, quoted in Lidstrom, 1991).

According to Lidstrom, in this broader definition of discretion organizations, or actors within those organizations, possess a certain scope for choice which is exercised within effective limits. In exercising their discretion actors take into account their own knowledge, judgement, assessment, beliefs and values.

Manley-Casimir (1991) has suggested that for many years the field and theory of education management have ignored the issue of discretion as an area for analysis and discussion. Instead the study of education administration has followed positivist traditions of value-free social scientific inquiry, drawing on organizational theory as its main discipline. Because of this, the notion of discretion, which is antithetical to the assumptions and methods of positivism, has largely been ignored.

Manley-Casimir argued that an examination of discretion should be a critical focus of study for those looking at education administration. In his view both education and education administration are value-based normative activities. Decision-making undertaken by key actors in the system cannot be divided into the rational and the intuitive. The exercise of judgement is central to the exercise of decision-making.

> Discretion is an authority conferred by law to act in certain conditions or situations in accordance with an official's or an official agency's own considered judgement and conscience. It is an idea of morals, belonging to the twilight zone between law and morals.
>
> (Pound, 1960, p. 926; quoted in Manley-Casimir, 1991)

In order to understand the significance of discretion in administration, Manley-Casimir suggested that concepts such as power, justice and responsibility needed clarifying and empirical and theoretical work on administrative decision-making from a variety of disciplines needed to be explored.

The issue of administrative discretion has engaged scholars from political theory, public administration, organizational theory, cognitive psychology, sociology, criminology and law. Political theorists have been concerned about discretionary power; criminologists with the presence of discretion in the justice system; administrative theorists with the exercise of discretion on a day-to-day basis. From these concerns two central issues have emerged, both of which are critical to our understanding of education administration: how to ensure that there are safeguards to prevent the abuse of power, and how to deal with the problems of bias in judgement.

> Discretion and its exercise is an absolutely central administrative process, ... it is quintessentially a human activity and hence not a property of organizations, ... it provides the bridge between empirical and normative, between fact and value in decision-making.
>
> (Manley-Casimir, 1991, p. 128)

Discretion is involved in the judgements and activities of educators at all levels of the system: from classroom teachers to chief education officers. How classroom teachers choose to exercise their discretion is pursued in some detail in Chapters 3 and 4. Education officers and elected members still have scope, even within the current context of the changes in educational powers and responsibilities, to exercise their discretion in ways that reflect the values and purposes of their organization.

A study of the exercise of discretion by local education authorities contrasted how very different LEAs chose to operate their discretion. One LEA used its discretion to maximize the redistribution of resources in pursuit of egalitarian goals:

> We believe that learning is a life-long process: it enables both individuals and society to grow and develop. The education service should help [the local area] to develop as a learning community which values its own cultural diversity. It should contribute to a more just and equal society. To do that, it needs to ensure that the opportunities and benefits of education are more equally shared.
>
> (Riley, 1992b, p. 13)

A second authority exercised its direction very differently: to develop its business planning activities in a way that would maximize market forces:

> [The objective is to] create the necessary conditions for fostering a system of vigorous self-management ... Institutions themselves will carry direct responsibility for delivering the planned services to the clients ... It is conceivable that this provision may have a contracted basis with the institutions themselves acting as client and purchasing assistance from LEA support services.
>
> (Riley, 1992b, p. 13)

One of the arguments in this book is that within the UK the *pursuit* of equal opportunities is largely a discretionary activity, although within a mandatory framework which forbids certain aspects of discrimination. Within this weak national framework, the key to equality of opportunity lies with the major actors in the education service: practitioners, policy-makers and governors. (How education 'consumers' will feature in this framework is as yet unclear.) These key actors can use their discretion to pursue equality, or not. Value concepts and judgements also inform different understandings about equality.

EQUALITY: A CONTESTABLE CONCEPT

Over the past decade, a number of large organizations in both the public and private sector – driven by various circumstances and pressures – have attempted to introduce equality programmes. In local authorities equality programmes have covered council employment policies and the delivery of services and have largely focused on issues of race, gender and disability. Some authorities have also included sexual orientation, class and/or age as further aspects of their policy.

As was suggested earlier, resource maximization and social justice have been the two main arguments used in Britain, and elsewhere, to persuade organizations to tackle inequality. Arguments about social justice prevailed in the 1970s and to a lesser extent in the 1980s. In a number of inner-city areas, black parents' groups were instrumental in forcing questions about racial discrimination (e.g. the disproportionate rates of suspensions, or expulsions, of black students) on to the political agenda. A number of urban authorities were also influenced in the 1980s by the election of a new breed of councillors committed to equalities issues and determined to see significant changes in how local authority decisions were made and resources allocated (Riley, 1992b). Many grass roots equality initiatives in education, particularly on gender, were influenced by the experience and activities of classroom teachers (Arnot, 1986).

The drive to develop equality programmes in local authority education services was also influenced by evidence of the continuing discrimination experienced by disadvantaged groups:

- Hidden discrimination continued in schools.
- Parental concerns about the schooling of black children helped put issues about race on the education agenda.
- Many black students continued to under-perform in examinations.
- Female students still had unequal access to higher education.
- Female staff employed in the education service had unequal employment opportunities.
- Women in the labour force were still segregated into low-paid occupations.
- The gap between women's and men's pay was higher in the UK than almost any other European Community country.

In the harsher economic climate of the late 1980s and early 1990s arguments about social resource maximization have found greater favour than arguments about social justice. Equal opportunities arguments about resource maximization within the education service have focused on ensuring that scarce educational resources are used effectively. Equality strategies in education have emphasized the need to develop the potential of all pupils; to retain skilled staff in the organization and increase their effectiveness; and to attract key staff to shortage areas. But equal opportunities is an ambiguous and contested concept based on differing values and assumptions. Attempts to introduce equality policies have frequently led to confusion, misunderstanding and conflict (Riley, 1990a).

Equal opportunity strategies have largely been premised on one of two interpretations of equality: *equality of opportunity* and *equality of outcome.* Each of these two approaches is based on differing assumptions about the nature of inequality, the action needed to tackle it and the goals. The liberal interpretation of equality, equality of opportunity, has been concerned with ensuring that the rules of the game (for employment, or access to courses, or examinations) are set out fairly. The assumption has been that rigorous administrative controls and formalized systems will ensure that fair play takes place and create the circumstances in which previously disadvantaged groups compete equally with other groups of students, or employees.

The more radical conception of equality, equality of outcome, has been concerned about widening access (to courses, or to employment) through action designed to redress past inequalities. It has been an essentially interventionist strategy aimed at redistributing resources and opportunities to disadvantaged groups. Its success or failure has been measured in terms of outcomes and the degree to which disadvantaged groups have achieved access to power and resources.

It has been suggested that both approaches are vulnerable to the accusation that they promise more than they can deliver but that elements of both are required for future developments (LGIU, 1991b). Be that as it may, it is obvious that the context for tackling inequality has shifted dramatically over the last few years. Public sector spending has gradually been reduced. Overall national spending on education, for example, has declined as a proportion of GDP over the past decade from 5.5 to 4.6 per cent (*The Guardian*, 15.5.92). Legislative and financial changes, in education and other areas of local government, have shifted power from local government to central government, and from local government to schools and institutions. The power to influence equality issues is increasingly with the new stakeholders in education: an issue discussed more fully in Chapters 2 and 7.

QUALITY AND EQUALITY

Quality and equality, as already stated, are not identical concepts, although they are interrelated. *Quality is about levels and standards: equality about power and resources.* A tension exists between the two which is based on values and ideology. Through the exercise of their discretion – based on values and judgements – key actors in the system can influence quality and equality outcomes in favour of different groups in the system (see Figure 1.3).

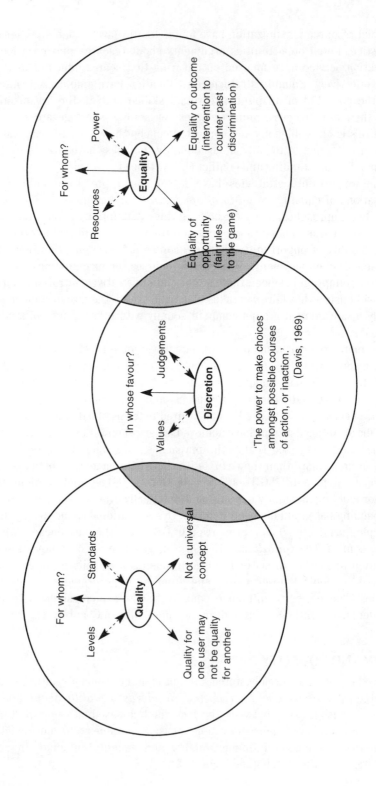

Figure 1.3   *Quality, equality and the exercise of discretion*

Posing the question *Quality for whom?* highlights the tension between quality and equality, and can result in radically different answers. At a time of financial constraints on public spending in education, the question of quality for whom becomes even more important.

- Is the objective of quality to further raise the standards of the high achievers in order to achieve limited economic imperatives?
- Is it to raise the standards of low achievers and move the UK up the economic league table?
- Is it to raise the standards and opportunities of particular groups of children: girls, black and ethnic minorities, children with disabilities?
- Fundamentally, is quality rooted on assumptions about universal standards, or on the rights of particular groups?

This book will argue that the notion of quality should also embrace a concept of equal opportunities which is focused not just on outcomes but on processes – *how* students experience and participate in the education system. Fundamental to this argument is the assertion that the organization and delivery of education services is more than the creation of a product for consumption.

Definitions of quality in education need to include consideration of standards but they also need to consider:

- Who is using the service?
- What are the range and diversity of needs?

If the providers of education services are driven to assuming that their goal is to achieve a common and standard service for all pupils, then we may well see the creation of an education service which is only suitable for a small number. A standard service may focus narrowly on the needs of middle-class, able-bodied white males, thereby ignoring the majority of students: female, black and ethnic minorities, people with disabilities. The organization and delivery of education needs to cater for diversity and changing needs: recognizing the individuality of students and those who deliver education services. A focus on quality and equality engaging those who are involved in education as users and as producers enables this complex process to take place.

> For all groups in society, access to influence and control over education, its contents and methods, is as important a dimension of equality with other groups as any quantitative measure of educational attainment. If equal participation in education by different groups will have any meaning as a measure of equality in educational terms, a precondition must be that the groups have equal share in deciding what education shall be about.
>
> (Eide, 1978)[2]

NOTES

1. There have been suggestions, for example, that the CBI intends to abandon support for equal opportunities for women and ethnic minorities and policies aimed at helping the disabled, the long-term unemployed, the over-50s and ex-offenders. A confidential report by CBI officials (leaked to a newspaper) argued that rising unemployment had reduced the need for employers to concern themselves with the under-representation of particular groups in the workforce. The 'demographic timebomb' – which had been expected to lead to a shortage of young people in the labour market – had been 'defused' (*The Independent on Sunday*, 14.2.93).

2. Quoted in OECD (1989).

Chapter 2

Education: the shift from egalitarianism to competition

TWO ACTS – BUT A WORLD APART

The 1944 Education Act was drawn up during the turmoil of the 1939–45 war. Its underlying egalitarian ethos was based on a broad political and establishment consensus and a belief that the social order of the day needed to be challenged.[1] The Archbishops of York, Canterbury and Westminster and the Moderator of the Free Church Council outlined the new agenda in a letter to *The Times*, in December 1940, entitled, 'Foundation for Peace'. The contributors argued that extreme inequality of wealth should be abolished and Disraeli's two nations, rich and poor, needed to be bridged. This view was echoed by leading politicians of the time: 'Every child regardless of race or class should have equal opportunities suitable for the development of his [*sic*] particular capabilities.' (Butler, 1973, p. 3).

Some 40 years later, in the run-up to the 1988 Education Reform Act, Kenneth Baker, Secretary of State for Education argued: 'The days of egalitarianism are over.'[2] How had such a radical shift come about? Why did egalitarianism no longer feature as a major objective of the education system?

The 1944 Education Act had a vision of secondary school opportunities for all children. Gone would be the days when only the most wealthy and able progressed to secondary education, whilst the bulk of children finished their final years of schooling (up to 14) as senior children in an all-age school. The 1944 Act paved the way for a new organizational framework – the tripartite system of grammar, technical and modern schools – and local authorities were required to submit their secondary school reorganization plans to the Secretary of State for Education, within this framework. A new system emerged in which children were to be tested at 11, through the '11 plus', and allocated to one of the three types of schools according to their 'aptitude and ability'. In practice, however, the new system became bipartite, rather than tripartite, as local authorities were reluctant to develop technical schools, largely because of their cost.[3]

By the 1950s there was a growing critique of the tripartite system. It was argued that the selective system at 11 reinforced class divisions in society and resulted in a 'wastage of ability'. Critics suggested that early streaming reflected social class much more than ability; that the tripartite system created 'a substantial reserve of uneducated ability in the offspring of the working-class' and that egalitarian goals could be achieved through a move to comprehensive education (Vernon, 1957; Floud, 1961).

The first purpose-built comprehensive school was opened in 1954, and by the early 1960s, although the issue was still controversial, there was growing support for the development of comprehensive education. By 1964 71 per cent of all local authorities had either established, or were planning to establish, this form of education (Rubinstein and Simon, 1969).

In October 1964 a Labour government was elected on a programme which included a commitment to introduce comprehensive schools. Michael Stewart, the Secretary of State for Education, issued the 10/65 Circular, which declared the government's intention to eliminate 'separatism in secondary education'.

Despite the major organizational shift from grammar and secondary to comprehensive schools, the decentralized education framework established by the 1944 Act continued throughout the 1960s. It was a framework which emphasized professional responsibility for educational outcomes and the centrality of the relationship between teacher and pupil. The educational professionals were the arbiters of educational performance – their judgements verified by the external examination bodies. Responsibility for performance lay with local education authorities, schools themselves, teacher-training institutions and to some extent with Her Majesty's Inspectorate. Education was considered to be a general good, although little national information was required about outcomes – apart from external examination results. A degree of uniformity across the system was assumed. The major national education goal was to produce a more educated labour force and nation.

By the early 1970s the emphasis was on the expansion of educational opportunities as the primary method of achieving these labour market goals. In 1972, as part of this expansionist thrust, Margaret Thatcher, as Secretary of State for Education, produced *A Framework for Expansion*, a White Paper on the expansion of nursery education, teacher supply and school buildings. But the subject of performance or standards did not feature in the White Paper; politicians did not consider such matters their responsibility. Accountability for performance was firmly within the domain of the educational professionals.

THE AGENDA FOR QUALITY

National concerns about quality in the UK and internationally emerged in the 1960s and 1970s. They stemmed from a view, shared by a number of governments, that the rapid extension of education in the 1960s and 1970s had failed to generate wealth and realize social equality (OECD, 1989).

Governments approached this problem in different ways. In the UK political scepticism about the quality of education had begun to emerge in the 1970s, reflected in publications such as the Black Papers on Education. The late 1970s and early 1980s saw a sustained, predominantly right-wing critique of education, which asserted that comprehensive education had brought about a lowering of standards (Ranson and Thomas, 1989). Both the goals and organization of education became subjected to political scrutiny and review. At the heart of these challenges was the belief that the educational professionals and local politicians were responsible for the failure of the education system.

Whilst Labour politicians did not share some of these perceptions, nevertheless they too held major reservations about the impact of expansionist education policies and were concerned about the high rates of youth unemployment and the number of young people leaving school without qualifications. James Callaghan's Ruskin Speech in 1976 offered a fundamental critique of state education: he deemed it to have failed to respond to technological change and the needs of employers. Callaghan's intervention proved to be something of a watershed: questions about quality, achievement and curriculum began to appear on the national agenda.

The election of a radical Conservative government in 1979 and the re-election of successive Conservative administrations cemented this shift in the debate. It also heralded the end to the liberal consensus in education. The discipline of the marketplace was to be introduced to ensure efficiency and counter egalitarianism.

The new government set out to challenge professional and producer control in education and in other public services. Accountability for educational performance was to be shifted from the educational professionals to central government and to consumers. The case for such a major shift in accountability was put forward by Kenneth Baker, Secretary of State for Education, as he introduced what was to become the 1988 Education Reform Act to the House of Commons.

> We must give consumers of education a central place in decision-making.
> That means freeing schools and colleges to deliver standards that parents
> and employers want. It means encouraging the consumer to demand that
> all educational bodies do the best job possible. In a word it means choice.
>   (House of Commons, 1987)

Professionals were to become accountable to consumers through the education marketplace and the application of consumer choice. Parents were to be given the opportunity to judge the effectiveness of schools through the provision of information about school performance on attainment targets and examination results. The dominant role of local authorities in the delivery of educational services was to be curtailed. Quality in education was to become a national goal.

The charge put forward by central government was that schools – and in particular comprehensive schools – had failed because they had pursued egalitarian goals at the expense of efficiency and effectiveness. Local education authorities were accused by central government of not having made the pursuit of quality a major objective. Central government asserted its views about quality through the introduction of the national curriculum and attainment tests. Market mechanisms were put into place through the development of new types of schools (grant-maintained schools and city technology colleges) and increased competition between schools. In 1992 a new semi-privatized inspection procedure was introduced. Consumer choice and accountability were the underlying elements of the new market-based education system (Riley, 1992b).

The main bones of the new education framework were established by the 1988 Education Reform Act. The Act brought about a marked change in the balance of power between central government and local government, and between local authorities and the schools and institutions in their locality. Central government acquired increased powers, largely at the expense of local authorities.

The 1988 Act had major consequences for schools and colleges. Headteachers and governing bodies assumed greater responsibilities for the financial management of schools and for the implementation of the National Curriculum. The Act paved the way for the introduction of grant-maintained schools which – following a parental ballot – could remove themselves from local authority control and receive direct funding from central government. Headteachers of grant-maintained schools and their governing bodies acquired considerable autonomy and direct responsibility for the employment of staff within their schools and for the allocation of resources.

The Act also removed further education from the remit of local authorities, creating a new incorporated status for colleges. However, college principals became subject to a new range of specific requirements from the Funding Council for Further Education (FCFE) on issues such as finance and measurement of institutional performance. College principals, headteachers and governors of grant-maintained schools thus acquired a greater degree of autonomy than their counterparts in schools maintained by local authorities.

With the increased politicization of education – and less national consensus about goals – questions about quality have remained high on the political agenda. The debate in the 1990s has continued with assertions from national government that standards have fallen: a charge denied by Eric Bolton, ex-Chief of Her Majesty's Inspectors of Education (Bolton, 1992).

Despite the continued disagreement about standards, it is clear that levels of educational achievement in the UK are lower than those of our industrial competitors. Such comparisons are evident, for example, in an economic analysis carried out by Kleinwort Benson Securities (1991) which draws on comparative OECD information to trace the relationship between educational attainment and 'economic misery' (a combined measure of the inflation and employment rates of a country). The study locates the UK as a high scorer on the 'economic misery' league table, near 'the bottom of the OECD class'. It argues that although, compared with other OECD countries, a relatively high proportion of the UK labour force possess a degree or equivalent, the UK will be unable to tackle 'economic misery' until it raises the educational achievement levels of those who leave school at 16. Whether this criticial issue will be remedied by the legislation of the past decade remains to be seen.

MARKETS, CHOICE AND DIVERSITY

In creating greater autonomy for schools and colleges, the 1988 Act substantially reduced the power and influence of the local education authority and created a 'privatization of education values'. Value choices which had formerly been made by the democratically elected local education authorities were handed over to schools and colleges (Ball, 1992). Following the 1988 Act the limitations of markets models for education services became increasingly apparent. Such limitations are likely to increase.

Cordingley (1992), for example, has argued that the imposition of market models on public sector organizations has seriously challenged the nature of local democracy. Market mechanisms cannot deliver on functions which are essential to the local governance of education such as:

- sustaining a sense of local community in education;
- the resolution of conflicting values and interests;
- developing the ability of people to be involved in decisions which affect their local community;
- providing involvement in collective decision-making; and
- developing mechanisms for accountability to the community as a whole.

Walsh (1992) has similarly highlighted some further limitations of the market model for education by suggesting that in a system based on individualistic rights, individuals may not be able to choose effectively. Market prices, such as the cost of private education, or charges for out-of-school visits or for music tuition, may exclude them, as may lack of knowledge about the system itself. He suggests that there are other limitations of national policy. Central government has also increasingly used contracts and charters as mechanisms for furthering its notion of citizenship – one based on individual rights – and as part of its new approach to the management of public service.

According to Walsh, *charters* state the rights and duties of the various parties involved and *contracts* clarify the nature of the relationship between the user and the provider. But *rights* guaranteed through charters are essentially guarantees of process, not guarantees of outcome. The Parent's Charter guarantees the right of parents to know what is taught, but not the right to influence it. Parents have the right to state a school preference, the right to appeal if that preference is not satisfied, but not the right of access to that school, or the right to certain levels of performance.

Given the new and evolving framework based on individual rights, the issue for the future is how far the new emphasis on markets, choice and diversity is compatible with notions of fairness and equity. What will be the opportunities for disadvantaged groups? Which parents will best be able to exercise their rights?

Questions also arise about the capacity of the suppliers (schools) to meet the needs of customers (parents and pupils). Will market pressures bring about greater similarity or greater diversity between schools? How different will well-resourced popular schools be from their less popular and under-resourced rival schools?

Brown (1990) has suggested that meritocracy has now been replaced by 'parentocracy' as the guiding principle: the wealth and power of parents is paramount in deciding which schools children attend and what their educational chances are. Arnot (1991), however, argues that concerns about public accountability and choice are not incompatible with social justice, an issue that is explored further in Chapter 6. The suggestion will there be made that there are real opportunities to use the debate about public performance and accountability to draw attention to issues of access and opportunities for particular groups of children.

Undoubtedly, the new framework established by the Education Reform Act has had major consequences for equality of opportunity. The rest of the chapter will examine the extent to which such equality has been enhanced, or diminished, by the legislative changes.

EQUALITY POST-EDUCATION REFORM ACT 1988

Table 2.1 Equal opportunities and the Education Reform Act 1988

	Encouraging equality	*Discouraging equality*
1. National Curriculum	Common curriculum experience Fewer girls drop science, fewer boys languages	Ignores hidden curriculum No parallel national push on impact of teachers' expectations, styles, resources on performance of black and ethnic minority pupils and girls Teachers may drop collaborative learning styles (which tend to benefit girls) in favour of more didactic styles (which favour boys)
2. National assessment	Limited yardstick to see how black and ethnic minority children/girls are faring	Teacher assessment of children (will black children and girls lose out?) Move to multiple-choice questions offers benefits to boys rather than girls
3. Local management of schools (employment)	Labour market pressure may open up opportunities for women, black and ethnic minorities and people with disabilities	Higher costs of women returners, cf. probationers, maternity leave, disabled access Financial management is 'men's business' Vulnerability of temporary staff
4. Local management of schools (financial)	Governors may place high emphasis on meeting community needs	Governors may redistribute resources from non-statutory sector (e.g. under-fives) to statutory
5. Grant-maintained schools		Covert selections Which children will be seen as highly motivated?
6. Open enrolment	Could force schools to be clearer about their goals More accountable for their outcomes	'Choice' only available to some parents. Could result in 'sink' schools in inner-city areas Escalation of 'Dewsbury' type situations

Gender equality

As a significant plank in the government's platform on quality, the 1988 Education Reform Act introduced a National Curriculum – creating significant changes for the content of teaching and learning.

But the demand for a common curriculum was not new: for many years feminists had argued that a common curriculum experience was a prerequisite to the achievement of classroom equality. Such arguments were based on egalitarian goals:

> Equality means the same – a common curriculum. But it is important to distinguish between the *overt curriculum* (the subjects and content of subjects offered to pupils) and the *hidden curriculum* (the largely unconscious attitudes, assumptions and practices of teachers towards their pupils).
>
> From the nursery upwards, it is essential that all children are offered a common curriculum (both overt and covert). In nursery and primary this means common play activities, craft lessons and the opportunities to learn skills. It also means ensuring that neither school organization, nor teacher expectations, differentiate between girls and boys.
>
> In secondary schools, we need to implement the comprehensive ideal and ensure that all children experience a curriculum which is undifferentiated. We must first decide what we think all children ought to know. And secondly, we must redefine existing subject areas in such a way that 'traditionally' female and male subjects disappear.
>
> Up to the end of compulsory education, a broad and balanced education with experience in all the major areas of learning, is essential for everyone ... At all levels, the common curriculum challenges the current system of option choices which is divisive in terms of subject choices and in terms of final examination selection (O level/CSE).
>
> (Benn et al., 1982)

Despite this support for a common curriculum, educators expressed early concerns about whether the form and content of the National Curriculum, as outlined in the 1988 Act, would contribute to gender equality. These concerns sprang from the apparent lack of awareness of, or focus on, equality issues in the Department of Education and Science documents on the Education Reform Act.

The National Curriculum outlined in the 1988 Act promised curriculum entitlement for all English and Welsh pupils, but concentrated only on formal access to the curriculum, ignoring the hidden curriculum. Even the formal entitlement to the National Curriculum was limited. An amendment dropped the original proposal that 20 per cent of the school week of 4th- and 5th-year secondary pupils be spent on a broad and balanced science programme, in favour of an option which allowed pupils to spend 10 per cent of their time on a single science subject. The two-tier system which was developed created a science hierarchy in which boys were more likely to choose the 20 per cent option and girls the 10 per cent option: a decision which would ultimately restricts girls' access to other educational levels.

The National Curriculum placed great store on the lack of differentiation. But it ignored the daily informal life of the school, which provides children with very differentiated experiences – as Chapters 3 and 4 will demonstrate. It failed to tackle the problems of race and gender disadvantage in schools, offering little on the important factors that underpin change, such as in-service training or school development planning. By ignoring the school processes, it served to legitimate hidden discrimination. A common curriculum experience may be a necessary, but it is not a sufficient, condition for gender equality.

The changes provoked many criticisms. Miles and Middleton (1990) argued that the National Curriculum concentrated only on the formal provision of equal access, ignoring gender divisions and inequalities. Kant (1987) argued that although the National Curriculum held the prospect of an undifferentiated curriculum, in practice it would only serve to confirm girls' views of themselves as second-class citizens, in a world where low-status 'female' subjects such as child-care were non-compulsory and 'male' science subjects were given high status.

Other writers have suggested that stereotyping in teacher assessment may create problems for both black pupils and girls when they are being assessed for the Standard Assessment Tasks – SATs (Gipps, 1990). Riddell (1992), for example, has pointed to past research evidence which shows the negative consequences on girls' opportunities of teachers' assumptions. Girls and boys who did equally well in mathematics were differentially allocated to O level and CSE groups. In explaining this decision, teachers described girls as 'not really bright' and 'working to their full potential' whilst boys were characterized as 'really bright' but 'underachieving' (Walden and Walkerdine, 1985).

There have also been criticisms of the lack of attention paid to the subject of equality by the various task groups which set up the National Curriculum and Standard Assessment Tests. Certainly, the working groups failed to acknowledge that the organization of subject knowledge could have profound consequences for teaching and learning. Gipps (ibid.) criticized the report of the task groups on assessment and testing in 1987 for devoting only 21 lines to bias and equal opportunities. Other researchers, such as Arnot (1989), noted the absence of women and black and ethnic minorities from the working groups. Arnot also argued that equal opportunities was defined merely as a matter of implementation, with an underlying assumption that teachers had high expectations about race and gender. Certainly, the question of training and support for teachers in tackling inequalities were largely ignored by the task groups.

More recently, concerns have also been expressed that girls will lose out as a result of the switch from more complex tests to short written tests for 14-year-olds. Results from the pilot National Curriculum tests in 1991 showed girls doing better than boys in mathematics and science – subjects where boys have traditionally been the higher scorers (*Times Educational Supplement*, 29.11.92). Girls also scored higher in English and technology: a position which may be reversed by changes in the tests. Pressures on teachers to ensure that pupils reach attainment targets may also mean that collaborative learning styles (which are known to favour girls) are dropped in favour of more direct teaching methods.

In a limited number of areas, however, the National Curriculum Council has advocated a positive stance on equal opportunities. In its publications on work experience, for example, the Council took the following line of argument.

> All pupils regardless of culture, gender or social background, should have access to a curriculum which promotes economic, and industrial understanding. Schools should be aware of pupils' attitudes and assumptions which relate to this component of the curriculum, for example, gender stereotypes about technology as a subject and engineering as a career. Programmes for economic and industrial understanding should explore and combat these stereotypes.
>
> (National Curriculum Council, 1990)

In general, however, it seems that the National Curriculum is unlikely to be a positive force in promoting gender equality.

> [The National Curriculum's] many transformations since inception suggest that it will probably look fairly similar to the previous option-choice system ... a range of vocational courses will continue to co-exist alongside National Curriculum subjects, and these two are sex-stereotyped.
>
> (Riddell, 1992, p. 51)

Table 2.1 (p. 22) summarizes some of the equal opportunities implications of the Education Reform Act 1988 for pupils and staff, highlighting those features of the Act which could provide a push towards equality (e.g. the National Curriculum) and those which represent a movement away from equality (e.g. the lack of focus on the hidden curriculum).

Racial equality

Concerns have also been expressed about the extent to which the Education Reform Act offers a vehicle to challenge racism; it may rather compound racial inequality. The National Curriculum has been criticized for promoting a white Anglo-Saxon Christian culture at the expense of ethnic minority cultures, languages and religions.[4] There have also been concerns that the emphasis on parental choice could result in some parents rejecting schools because of the presence of black children, as happened in Dewsbury.

Particular concerns have focused on the extent to which race issues have become increasingly marginalized through the overall impact of legislative changes. Taylor (1992) conducted a survey of all local authorities (two-thirds of which replied) that examined whether the Education Reform Act had impeded or enhanced equal opportunities and the provision of multicultural and anti-racist education.

Although two-thirds of the respondents to the survey reported some 'progress', Taylor highlighted the point that one-third of the respondents had reported that multi-cultural and anti-racist practices had stultified or declined – particularly in the London area. Interviewees attributed this lack of progress to the pressures of the Education Reform Act: schools were preoccupied with the National Curriculum and assessment, local education authorities with their survival. There was also a shared perception amongst interviewees that 'The national education and political climate was ideologically unpropitious to multi-culturalism and anti-racism' (Taylor, ibid., p. 5).

Women staff and equality

The effects of the Education Reform Act 1988 and the Education Act 1993 on equality for staff are complex but the two major issues are: have the capacities of staff been developed to tackle inequalities, and have employment opportunities for female staff been enhanced or diminished by legislation? On the issue of the training and development of staff, De Lyon and Widdowson Migniuolo (1989) have argued that although the 1988 Act itself fails to focus on teachers' development, there is still considerable scope to develop the capacity of teachers to deal with equality issues. For this to happen, teacher educators must address gender issues at all stages – from initial teacher training to in-service training (INSET) – if teachers are to be equipped to challenge rather than to reinforce inequalities. Teacher training needs to provide, for example, a systematic analysis of how sex stereotyping influences school life and also to explore the causes and consequences for the education service of the under-representation of women in education management.

The second issue – the extent to which employment opportunities have been enhanced or diminished by legislation – needs to be examined in the broader context of the realignment of powers brought about by the Education Reform Act. Local management of schools has transferred the responsibility for setting the budget, for deciding curriculum priorities and for appointing staff from local authorities to governors and headteachers. The issue also needs to be explored within the context of past discrimination against women.

Such discrimination has covered a number of areas. The ban on married women teachers was only gradually removed during the 1930s. As mentioned in note 1, equal pay for women staff was one of the few contentious issues in the 1944 Education Act and was not in fact achieved until 1961. With a few exceptions, women have only been appointed to headteacher positions in coeducational schools within the past half-century. Entrenched views opposed such advancement. The appointment of a woman to the headship of a school (even one without senior children) received the following reaction in one shire county in the 1940s:

> Objections to a woman being selected as head of a school was voiced by the Thorne education sub-committee when they considered a letter from the West Riding county education committee, stating that they proposed to appoint a woman head to succeed Mr J. W. Page, retiring head at Hatfield Travis School.

The sub-committee, in a resolution urging the county to reconsider that decision, pointed out that it would be the first time in living memory that a woman has held the position in the school.

With the removal of the senior children to the modern school, the school now has only infant children.

(*Education*, 12 February 1943)[5]

The issue today is how the recent shift in powers to appoint and promote staff, from local authorities to governing bodies, will affect opportunities for women. Will local management of schools increase or decrease the number of women appointed to headships?

As yet the evidence is sketchy but unpromising. In the state of Victoria, Australia, the delegation of powers of appointment of headteachers to school boards in the late 1980s had led to a reduction in the number of women appointed as headteachers. Certainly, as will be discussed in Chapter 5, there is growing evidence to suggest that the characteristics that are associated with successful management of the education service are becoming more, rather than less, associated with men than women. The new financial and organizational responsibilities required by local management of schools (LMS) are resulting in senior appointments increasingly being seen as 'men's business'.

In making their decisions, governing bodies are also constrained by growing financial restrictions, a problem exacerbated by the fact that schools receive average rather than actual salary costs. There are some worrying indications that women staff – particularly those with family and caring responsibilities – may be losing out.

Evidence of this shift is reflected in a longitudinal study on the impact of local management of schools (Bullock, Thomas and Arnott, 1993). Headteachers interviewed in the study expressed growing concern about appointing experienced, and therefore relatively expensive, staff to posts. Such staff are often likely to be women returners. The study, which covered 467 schools, also found an increase in the employment of staff, particularly part-time staff, on temporary contracts. Part-time staff are predominantly female. In 1990 the schools had 38 per cent of part-time staff on temporary contracts; in 1991 the proportion had increased to 54 per cent. This trend results from budgetary uncertainties. Its adverse consequences for staff include lowered morale and reduced career and developmental opportunities. Such factors must ultimately impinge on classroom activities, as will any loss to the education service of experienced returners.

Local authorities and equality

A critical question for the future is how effectively will local education authorities be able to support equal opportunity – for staff and pupils – in all its aspects. Over the past decade the power of authorities has diminished along with the number of areas in which they can intervene. Interviewees in the Taylor (1992) study expressed their concerns about whether the local authority would be able to support schools in the development of effective race policies.

The lack of a national, or any local authority, database to monitor the equality implications of this major new legislative framework is also a cause for concern. Indeed, the education authority which had the fullest database and monitoring procedures on equality – the Inner London Education Authority (ILEA) – was abolished by the 1988 Act without such a database, key questions and issues of equality will remain largely unanswered (see Chapter 6).

TENSIONS AND DILEMMAS IN THE EDUCATION SYSTEM

Tensions and dilemmas in the education system became apparent soon after the implementation of the 1988 Act. Problems connected with school admissions became critical, as the scope for local authorities to plan for sufficient school places in their locality and to administer a system for allocating those places was eroded. This planning blight was brought about by the creation of grant-maintained schools and city technology colleges (both of which were free to establish their own admissions criteria); by the reluctance of local authorities to implement school reorganization plans in order not to precipitate an increase in opt-out schools; and by the Greenwich judgment.[6]

Tensions reached a peak in 1992, highlighting the limitations of the new education market mechanisms. There was evidence to suggest, for example, that grant-maintained schools were increasingly selecting their pupils – by using academic, social or economic criteria – rather than parents selecting the schools. In a number of areas of the country the difficulties of secondary school transfer were exacerbated by the new education marketplace. In Hillingdon, for example, which had four grant-maintained schools at the time, more than 100 children were not offered secondary school places for a period of months. Parental choice became more of an aspiration than a reality (*Times Educational Supplement*, 31.1.92 and 5.6.92).

The government's argument was that these changes were in response to parental concerns about the state of education. Undoubtedly many parents held strong views about developments in the education service, but parental views appeared to focus on basic standards in education rather than on issues of choice. A survey of some 4,000 parents and adult education students carried out in March 1992, for example, found that 62 per cent of primary school parents rated standards of reading, writing and arithmetic as their major educational concern, followed by discipline and truancy (38 per cent) and 'the rapid rate at which reforms to the systems have been introduced' (18 per cent). Parents wanted smaller classes, better trained and better paid teachers, more books and equipment and better maintained school buildings (*TES*, 3.3.92).

These parental concerns emanated from the financial constraints which many schools and local authorities were facing. The increased selectivity of grant-maintained schools, on top of the preferential financial treatment given to them – a capital grant of £231 per pupil, compared with £109 for pupils in local authority maintained schools, plus a one-off transitional grant of £60,000 (1991/92 figures) – were creating new inequalities and social divisions in local education services. Continued controls on local authority spending by central government, coupled with local management of schools intensified the financial pressures on governing bodies, which also had to struggle to meet the national teachers' pay settlement of 7.8 per cent on local budget increases of around 5 per cent (*The Guardian*, 1992).[7] In 1992, 7,000 teaching and lecturing posts were lost as well as thousands of part-time jobs, resulting in a 1.4 per cent drop in teaching staff and a 1 per cent drop in other education staff (*The Guardian*, 18.1.1993).

Along with evidence that grant-maintained schools were increasingly choosing their pupils came the suggestion that local authority maintained schools were increasingly excluding pupils.[8] As schools lost their support systems and became more publicly accountable for their performance on examination results and Standard Assessment Tests, the presence of disruptive children within a school became even more problematic.

The year 1991–2 also witnessed a power struggle – between governors and the headteacher – at Stratford (grant-maintained) School in the East End of London, which culminated in a protracted legal battle and direct intervention by the Secretary of State for Education, through the appointment of additional governors to the school. The Stratford school débâcle highlighted a further major tension in the system: the lack of external controls on grant-maintained schools and their governing bodies. It opened up the possibility that power – in this case that exercised by the governing body – could be misused.

It was in response to some of these difficulties that in 1992 a Conservative administration, re-elected earlier in the year to its fourth term in office, introduced another Education Bill, building on proposals set out in the Education White Paper *Choice and Diversity: A New Framework for Schools* (HMSO, 1992). This became the 1993 Education Act and represented a further erosion of the powers and responsibilities of local authorities. It sought to encourage specialization and the development of more grant-maintained schools. It established an 'evolutionary framework' for the future, partly through the Funding Agency for Schools (FAS), set up to share responsibility for education planning with local authorities, depending on the proportion of grant-maintained schools in a locality. Whether specialization will turn into selection and whether bureaucracy and duplication will increase or diminish, as yet remains unclear.

Many sceptics remain to be convinced that the Act will provide the education framework needed for the future. A leader in the *Financial Times*, for example, commented on the proposals in the White Paper:

> Schools are in for a huge, generation-long bureaucratic reshuffle. The connection between this upheaval and the theory of parental choice is evident. The connection with the improvement of what goes on in the classroom is not.
>
> (*Financial Times*, 29.7.92)

The 1993 Act certainly continues the process of fragmentation of local education services (although probably not the end of local authority involvement in education). New organizational patterns will develop which will be influenced by local choices and circumstances. New tensions are also likely to emerge as a consequence of these power realignments, and new stakeholders – who are increasingly located in non-elected agencies – will become key players in the local governance of education.

How local authorities have responded to the changes since 1988 may throw some light on the likely impact and consequences of the 1993 Act. In a research study which draws on the experience of three local education authorities with very distinct purposes, Cordingley and Kogan (1993) have argued that although local authorities have adapted to the legislative pressures in different ways, there are some common elements. All three local authorities in their study shared fundamental changes in the values to which they subscribed, and the needs, or functions, which they increasingly discounted.

The study suggested (pp. 32–3) that the values newly emphasized were:

> Individual choice, institutional autonomy, deference to nationally determined standards of excellence (through inspection, testing and nationally prescribed curricula)

and that the needs, or functions, increasingly discounted were

> local variation, equity, choices of forms of quality assurance (e.g. self-evaluation), detailed intervention, specification or purchase of local education provision.

What these shifts re-emphasize is that the days of direct and detailed intervention by local authorities in the policies and practices of schools have ended. What remains, however (see Chapters 6 and 7), is the scope for influence. Although the local authorities no longer have direct control over headship appointments, they can influence recruitment through the training and advice given to governors. Grant-maintained schools, although even more firmly outside the remit of local authorities, are not automatically immune to their influence, or closed to equality issues (Lord, 1992).

The legislation pushes schools towards increased isolation, forcing them to compare their performance on public examinations and national tests with that of other schools. This competitive climate will have the effect of discouraging staff and governors from asking open questions about how particular groups – girls or boys, black or white children — are performing in their school as compared with the same groups in other, comparable schools. Local authorities can play a key role in countering this isolation and providing a framework for considering issues of equality (see Chapters 6 and 7).

Detailed intervention on equality is no longer possible but the opportunity still exists for authorities to retain equality as a valued policy objective. A director of education, referring to the role and purposes of his authority, said:

In many ways equality of opportunity is a major area of discretion for LEAs but for us it is our main purpose. Equality of opportunity is core to notions of learning and to the way the curriculum is constructed.

(Riley, 1992a, p. 13)

The next chapter will examine the extent to which equality of opportunity has been central to core notions of teaching and learning. It looks back to the years before the legislation of the 1980s and 1990s, to explore whether the education framework established over the past century has provided equal access and equal opportunities for children. What have been the processes and outcomes of schooling?

NOTES

1. The 1944 Act was introduced into the House of Commons with cross-party support. One of the few areas of political disagreement was on the issue of equal pay for women.
2. Statement made by Kenneth Baker in introducing the Education Reform Act to an education conference in 1987 (quoted in Riddell and Brown, 1992).
3. By 1958 technical schools took only 4 per cent of the relevant age group and many authorities had no technical schools (Rubinstein and Simon, 1969).
4. See, for example, *Multicultural Teaching* **6** (1988) and *Issues in Race and Education* **56** (1989).
5. Reprinted in *Education* **181** (6), 12 February 1993.
6. The Greenwich legal judgment gave parents the right to choose a school in a neighbouring local authority. Nearnesss to the school was considered to be a higher priority than residence within a local authority area. The judgment has had the effect of reducing the capacity of local authorities to plan for school places for children within the local authority boundaries.
7. Although in a number of parts of the country there has been a decline in the student population, local authorities have been unable to benefit from planned reductions in school places for the reasons suggested earlier in the chapter.
8. A MORI study carried out for a BBC 'Panorama' television programme in March 1993 found that temporary or permanent exclusions from schools had risen by 50 per cent over two years and stood at 66,000 pupils per year.

PART II
THE EDUCATIONAL EXPERIENCE

Chapter 3

The educational experience

> Boys will be boys,
> It's a fact of human nature,
> And girls will grow up to be mothers.
> Leon Rosselson

INTRODUCTION

In this chapter I begin by reviewing the organization of education over the last century and showing how sex differentiation in schooling has reflected societal expectations about the roles of women and men – expectations which have also been class-related. My analysis suggests that inequalities are not an accident of history and that shifts in power relations are needed to bring about change. The changing patterns of inequality reinforce the importance of monitoring and processes and outcomes.

I then move on to explore the introduction of comprehensive education, suggesting that the generic views about quality that were presented by the supporters of comprehensive education – although springing from a strong egalitarian tradition – largely ignored issues of gender. Quality for all obscured analysis of the consequences of coeducation for girls.

Finally I suggest that analysis of the classroom experience of both girls and black students reminds us that through exercising discretion in critical areas teachers and schools *can* influence pupils' life chances.

The analysis presented in this chapter suggests that awareness of how race, gender and class impact on schooling remains confused. Where these issues have been tackled by researchers, or practitioners, they have been explored in isolation from each other: pupils have been seen as working class or female or black. There has been little examination of the inter-relationship between class, race or gender, yet the complex processes which affect schooling are influenced by all three.[1]

CLASS AND GENDER IN THE EDUCATION OF GIRLS

In the early nineteenth century, there was little differentiation in the limited education offered to working-class girls and boys (Silver and Silver, 1974). The education of upper-middle-class girls and boys was, however, highly differentiated: girls were encouraged to develop social accomplishments, boys academic success (Nava, 1984).

By the late nineteenth century, this picture had begun to change for both working-class and middle-class girls. There was increasing differentiation in the curriculum offered to working-class girls and boys. The curriculum for working-class girls became increasingly 'domesticated' and domestic economy became one of the specific subjects for which government grants were made – a development which reflected societal changes. Working-class women were expected to take on one of two servicing roles: either servicing male partners and children and fulfilling the ideal model of bourgeois, Victorian family life; or servicing the domestic requirements of the new entrepreneurial classes (Purvis, 1984; Nava, ibid.).[2]

For working-class girls, the domesticated curriculum was their only option. For most middle-class girls, private education provided the academic opportunities for a few but also created the social class solidarity that enabled them to get the 'right' husband. Some middle-class girls, however, had the opportunity of attending 'uncompromising' secondary schools, such as North London Collegiate, which provided rigorous academic opportunities and a possible avenue through university colleges such as Hitchin (later to become Girton) College, to the professions (Nava, ibid.). The domestic servicing function of working-class girls also freed those professional women from domestic labour (David, 1980; Nava, ibid.).

By the mid-twentieth century little had changed. The Norwood Report (1943) enshrined a view of women as homemakers and provided the rationale for post-war girls' education. The report included a lengthy chapter on domestic subjects (which included needlework, cookery, laundry and housekeeping), which were to be included in girls' education for three reasons: 'knowledge of such subjects is a necessary equipment for all girls as potential homemakers'; domestic subjects 'had the advantage of (offering) a practical approach to theoretical work'; and finally, domestic subjects could be a qualification requirement 'for girls likely to go on to Domestic Science Colleges'. 'For many girls it is felt that domestic subjects provide a centre of interest natural and congenial to them' (Norwood Report, pp. 127–8, quoted in David, 1980).

The Norwood Report also provided the ideological basis for the tripartite system of secondary schooling set up by the 1944 Education Act – a system which aimed to provide a degree of social class mobility.[3] Its ultimate effect, however, was to solidify class divisions, with secondary modern schools becoming virtually synonymous with working-class schooling and grammar schools with middle-class schooling (Floud, 1961; Rubinstein and Simon, 1969).

In the 1950s industrial pressures to increase productivity and train a more skilled workforce provided the impetus for an examination of the failure of the education system to develop the talents and skills of the future workforce. The Crowther Report (1959), which undertook this review, based its thinking on two fundamental assumptions: that the workforce was predominantly male and that secondary modern schools were particularly responsible for the wastage of talent. The curriculum recommendations made by Crowther in respect of modern schools were thus highly sex-differentiated, reinforcing the gender and class divisions of the labour market. Secondary modern schools were advised to make sufficient provisions for girls' interests in matrimony and domestic life:

> The prospect of courtship and marriage, should rightly influence the education of the adolescent girl ... her direct interests in dress and personal experience and the problems of human relationships, should be given a central part in her education.
>
> (Crowther, 1959, p. 124)

Grammar school girls, who were predominantly middle class, were excused the full excesses of the domesticated curriculum.

A NATION DIVIDED BY CLASS (AND GENDER?)

The Wilson Labour government of 1964 promised to challenge class divisions in state education through the introduction of comprehensive education. In July 1965 the government issued Circular 10/65, which declared its intention to end the separatism of the tripartite system and to create comprehensive schools, which would offer wider and less differentiated curriculum opportunities for all pupils (Rubinstein and Simon, 1969).

The primary focus of the debate in the 1960s about comprehensive education was class; issues of gender were largely ignored. 'Does comprehensive education necessarily imply coeducation? Some [local authorities] have thought so, others not' was the limit of the gender debate in one major study of comprehensive education (Rubinstein and Simon, 1969, p. 101). An earlier study gave the subject a little more attention; one paragraph dismissed the case for single-sex schooling in the following terms:

> More than half of London's new schools are for either boys or girls only ... the establishment of new schools on this one-sex basis is deplorable. They can at best only be semi-comprehensive. The real point of the argument for having a school which is a mixed, balanced, healthy, natural community is lost. Such lopsided experience, in an almost exclusively male or female world ... cannot be reconciled with the case for an education which is socially complete as well as scholastically sound.
>
> (Pedley, 1963, pp. 87–8)

The inter-relationship between disadvantage stemming from class and that stemming from gender is difficult to disentangle. The important point for the purposes of this chapter is to suggest that action to remove class disadvantage will not automatically help working-class girls, unless the gender disadvantages are also tackled. The search for class equality – if it is blind to such issues as gender and race – may improve the quality of the education experience for some children (white boys) at the expense of other groups. This issue is fundamental to the debate about quality and equality.

Education initiatives in the 1980s aimed at achieving class equality suffered from the same inadequacies. The Hargreaves Report, for example, analysed the under-achievement of working-class children and offered a radical rethinking of the definition of academic achievement. However, the Report gave limited attention to the educational experience of girls. Indeed, it suggested that the 'problem' of girls' lack of participation in science and technology was located in the pupil and made no recommendations on teacher re-education, parental involvement or curricular change (ILEA, 1984).

The late 1970s and early 1980s witnessed a fundamental challenge to the egalitarian goals of the comprehensive education system. But critics had already begun to challenge the gender weaknesses of the model in the late 1960s and early 1970s. The women's movement focused attention not only on the *outcomes* of education, employment and training but also on the *processes* (women's experience of education, training and employment). How girls and young women experienced their schooling – in single-sexed and coeducational schools – thus became a focus for research and analysis, and remains a highly controversial issue.

SINGLE-SEX OR COEDUCATIONAL?

The case for coeducation was put strongly by Dale (1969). He argued that both girls and boys from coeducational schools tended to have happier memories of their school lives than pupils from single-sex institutions and that coeducational schools provided better social adjustment for both sexes. He acknowledged, however, that the academic performance of boys in coeducational schools improved whilst that of girls declined. He argued that the fall in the academic performance of the girls was compensated by their increased maturity. Dale also held strong views about the nature of leadership in schools. 'Opinion in the country is not ready for more than the exceptionally good headmistress to be placed in charge of a mixed grammar school' (p. 228).

Dale's work did not go unchallenged. Shaw, for example, argued that the fall in the academic performance of girls in coeducational schools was not an acceptable trade-off for the 'mutual' social advantages for both sexes.

> The acceptable trade-off is supposed to be a poorer education for girls, in favour of a 'happier' marriage for both girls and boys and even more sex role stereotypes. Mixed schools are essentially boys' schools, in so far as they are dominated by boys' interests.
>
> (Shaw, 1980, p. 69)

Shaw (1984) went on to argue that the class divisions of the tripartite system had been replaced by class and gender divisions in comprehensive schools. Coeducation had failed to recognize, or take action against, gender inequality. While single-sex schooling for girls could provide the opportunity for gender solidarity, many of the options for single-sex schools were class-related as the remaining single-sex schools tended to be denominational, selective, or in the private sector.

The debate about the merits of coeducation and single-sex schooling continued throughout the 1980s. Brehoney (1984) argued that the coeducation propagandists (who in the first two decades of the century had been predominantly male) had inflated their claims for both the cognitive and social outcomes of coeducation. Historically there was a fragile case for coeducation. Brehoney distinguished between mixed schooling, i.e. the segregated schooling of girls and boys in the same building, which was already in existence in the nineteenth century, and coeducation. Coeducation aimed to remove artificial constraints and conventions between the sexes and took place in high status, well-resourced private progressive schools, whose influence and reputations were out of proportion to their numbers.

Researchers also focused on the academic performance of girls in single-sex and coeducational schools. Blackstone and Weinrich-Haste (1980) argued that girls performed better academically in single-sex than in coeducational schools, even in mathematics and science: areas in which traditionally boys had out-performed girls. In coeducational schools there was a greater polarization of girls into arts and boys into science. Other research supported these findings and indicated that once academic results have been adjusted for social class, girls in single-sex schools still out-performed girls in coeducational schools (ILEA, 1982; Rutter *et al.*, 1979).

Other research suggested that pupils in single-sex girls' schools concentrated more on the task 'in hand' than pupils in coeducational schools and expressed a greater degree of warmth and sympathy with their teachers (Bone, 1983). The absence of boys also enabled girls in single-sex schools to speak out and ensured that they were not subjected to sexual harassment (Shaw, 1980). However, there was also evidence to suggest that girls in mixed schools were significantly more likely to have enjoyed their schooling than girls in single-sex schools.

GIRLS' SUBJECTS AND BOYS' SUBJECTS

Gender issues in the curriculum and organization of school subjects first received official attention in the mid-1970s with the publication of an HMI survey (DES, 1975). The survey highlighted the different educational experiences offered to girls and boys in primary schools, secondary schools (both single-sex and coeducational) and further education. It focused on both the hidden and overt curriculum and argued that most of the gender divisions in the education system were unjustified and contributed to a 'wastage of talent':

> If all secondary schools were to carry out an analysis of both content and organisation from the first year onwards and to ensure that choices made later were based, as nearly as is practicable, on real equality of access to experience, to information and to guidance, that would be one step towards eradicating prejudices about the roles of men and women which frustrate individual development and cause a wastage of talent a country can ill afford.
>
> (DES, 1975, p. 24)

The survey reflected a very different social climate to that in which Crowther had prevailed some 16 years earlier. It was one in which women were considered to be part of the workforce and in which their skills were increasingly in demand. The

Equal Pay Act (1970) and the Sex Discrimination Act (1975) introduced by Labour governments to challenge discrimination against women reflected the changes in attitudes.

The HMI survey focused on the curriculum and option choice available in both coeducational and single-sex schools. It found that although girls were more likely to be offered a non-traditional girls' subject in a coeducational school, they were more likely to choose such a subject in a single-sex school. Later studies in the 1980s also found that the girls in single-sex schools were more favourably inclined to technology and industry – including technology as a school subject – than girls in coeducational schools (Page and Nash, 1980).

The HMI survey also found that in 98 per cent of the coeducational secondary schools reviewed, although girls and boys were taught together for some core subjects, many other subjects were highly differentiated by gender. This separatism was far removed from the strategies advocated by feminists such as Spender and Sarah (1980) – the separation of girls and boys for the teaching of mathematics, for example, to enable the girls to have a mathematical experience equivalent to that of boys; it was a differentiation based on the assumption that there are boys' subjects and girls' subjects.

THE HIDDEN CURRICULUM

The effect of this unequal experience of education was that girls were denied the opportunity to participate on equal terms in the labour market. Both the overt and the hidden curriculum contributed to this process of differentiation and discrimination. The hidden curriculum – the messages that are transmitted to pupils through schools' underlying practices – reflected expectations and assumptions about pupils which related to their ethnic origin, social class and gender. These assumptions and practices were (and perhaps still are) taken for granted in schools and were evinced in long-established forms of school administration and organization. (Chapter 4 will describe in some detail how the hidden curriculum affected the educational experience of young women in four London schools.)

A key element of the hidden curriculum has been its impact on the expectations of girls. Clarricoates (1980), for example, argued that primary schools defined constructs of 'femininity' and 'masculinity'. Expectations about the behaviour and norms for children were strictly sex-differentiated and went far beyond sexist reading schemes and segregation of pupils into sports, or craft activities, to clearly differentiated and gender-defined treatment of pupils by teachers. Clarricoates described how teachers characterized girls as obedient, tidy, neat, conscientious, orderly, fussy, catty, bitchy, gossiping and boys as livelier, adventurous, aggressive, boisterous, self-confident, independent, energetic, couldn't-care-less, loyal (ibid., p. 39).

For working-class girls, as was indicated in early discussions on the Crowther Report, class and gender have often been inter-related. Clarricoates also argued that working-class girls were pressurized into appropriate 'feminine' roles at an earlier age than middle-class girls, thereby limiting their educational horizons and ensuring that ultimately they entered the lowest rungs of the labour market. Similarly,

McRobbie (1978), in a study of working-class girls (carried out in the mid-1970s) suggested that schools reproduced – and ultimately working-class girls conformed to – a cult of feminity, although the girls were often aware of the limitations and contradictions of this cult within their own home lives.

GIRLS AND WOMEN IN THE 1990s

In the 1990s the issue of girls' experience in single-sex and coeducation has resurfaced following a survey by HMI (DFE, 1992). The survey, which was carried out during 1990 and 1991, involved eight secondary schools in two LEAs and was backed up by further evidence from 70 HMI studies of secondary schools. The purpose of the study was to examine how schools prepared girls for adulthood and their working lives.

> Statistics and reports point to the fact that although women now spend less time raising families before returning to work, they are less well represented than men in management positions; that fewer women than men are employed in scientific and mathematical occupations; that women account for the major part of the lower-paid work force in caring and support roles and the majority of part-time workers. A range of roles is undertaken by women and their quality of life depends on the ability to balance and accommodate the demands of these various roles. With this in mind the education of girls was chosen as the focus for a survey. Clearly many of the issues in the report have implications for the education of boys, as well as girls.
>
> (DFE, 1992, p. 1)

The survey found that in coeducational schools many teachers paid insufficient attention to the ways in which boys dominated the classroom. Teachers in mixed schools tended to assume that the presence of girls and boys ensured equal opportunities. In the view of HMI, many mixed schools failed to tackle equality issues and did not take advantage of the opportunity which they had to bring boys and girls together in discussions about shared and differing expectations.

> In mixed schools, generalised statements about boys and girls had an egalitarian flavour which in some places had the unfortunate consequence of disguising the specific needs of adolescent boys and girls.
>
> (ibid., p. 6)

HMI also noted, however, that the pattern within a school could be complex. Schools could hold two competing visions for girls: with some staff and departments working to enrich the educational experience of girls, whilst others regarded such activities as irrelevant.

The study found little careful monitoring of girls' and boys' achievement in mixed schools and a 'mistaken' view in two schools that 'having responded to equal opportunities by listing pupils alphabetically in registers and other documents, it would be against the spirit of equal opportunities to monitor performance separately'. The overall lack of analysis about pupil performance, interests, achievements and destinations in some of the coeducational schools meant that strategies for improvement for girls and boys could not be developed and also led to self-fulfilling prophecies about 'girls' ' and 'boys' ' subjects.

HMI found a consistently different picture in the single-sex girls' schools. Most schools had made positive assertions about the role of women, as in the extract from a booklet from one school:

> Today we know that being unable to support yourself is a risky way to live ... About a third of all marriages end in divorce and the divorce rate is rising rapidly ... The point, simply put, is that women need to be able to make enough money to support themselves ... It is now acceptable for a women to be anything from an astronaut to a zoo keeper. Your imagination and ambition are the only limitations.

> (ibid., p. 3)

The ethos of many of the girls' schools was established by 'forceful head-teachers' who used a range of leadership styles to bring about changes. Although a few of the single-sex schools believed that they provided better opportunities for girls simply by being single-sex this was not the norm. Most girls' schools had positive statements of their aims for girls such as:

> The single-sex environment ... offers opportunities for leadership and responsibility.

> When girls leave us we want them to be competent individuals with well-rounded human qualities.

> The aim of our school is to help all our girls to achieve success and to recognize that success, however it may be revealed.

HMI found that a higher proportion of lessons were challenging to girls in single-sex schools – encouraging them to think and apply knowledge – than in coeducational schools. Girls were also less likely to have low aspirations and stereotypical assumptions about the future in single-sex schools.

The survey aimed to gain the views of pupils in Years 9 to 13 about their schooling. Discussions with pupils therefore focused on such issues as:

- strengths and deficiencies of courses and curriculum;
- students' perception of their lives in ten years' time;
- decision-making processes and knowledge of alternative routes in education, training and employment;
- sources of help in school and outside;
- advantages and disadvantages of single-sex and mixed education;
- styles of teaching and learning;
- and opportunities to take responsibility and make decisions.

One group of girls in a single-sex school (which HMI described as particularly successful) described the ways in which their school had prepared them for their working life:

- they had learnt to get on with people;
- they had learnt to push themselves: 'You are required to work';
- they were not allowed to fall by the wayside (proper monitoring and tutoring): 'This school will not allow you to fail; but it does not over-protect – it is not a nanny';
- there was much encouragement to ask questions;
- teachers had high expectations;
- teachers did not put students down: 'They praise the good, but help with your weaknesses';
- they felt they could relate to most of the teachers: 'The teachers are not scared of a fight'; 'They will take the opposite point of view';
- they had developed positive attitudes to school and work;
- teachers had good knowledge of students: 'Students are made welcome by teachers and not left out';
- there was much encouragement to plan ahead.

(ibid., p. 14)

In reflecting on their schooling, girls in single-sex schools commonly argued that their schools had encouraged good science and mathematics and set high expectations for them – although pupils of average ability sometimes thought these expectations were too high. The girls recognized, however, a need to meet and work with boys and welcomed any opportunities which the school provided to encourage this. Girls in the survey, in both single-sex and coeducational schools, identified 'flexibility, confidence, inter-personal skills, team-building enthusiasm and leadership' as important qualities for effective working life.

The HMI study painted a picture of schooling for girls and boys which had changed little over the last two decades. The overwhelming finding was that girls' schools engendered self-confidence and high aspirations and expectations in their pupils. But what are the implications of the analysis provided by HMI? The survey certainly makes clear that gender issues have had limited impact in many schools and that – contrary to some assertions by Sheila Lawlor, deputy director of the Centre for Policy Studies – what she called 'discredited education orthodoxies' such as gender have not found their way into schools. Coeducational schools might no longer list girls and boys separately, but overall have gone little further in addressing inequalities.

But what about the boys? HMI also found that there was little evidence that boys' schools had considered the implications for boys' personal development of their status as single-sex schools. Few single-sex boys' schools included home economics as part of design and technology, or incorporated female perspectives into personal or health education courses. Boys in mixed schools dominated information technology courses and ignored child development. Boys – whether in single-sex or coeducational schools – were therefore not being equipped to take their responsibilities in caring, or to understand the changing role of women.

Yet schools can confront inequalities and help girls and boys to come to new shared understandings about their behaviour. The HMI study gave one example of how this can be undertaken and described a lesson with Year 11 pupils on equal opportunities in which the teacher divided the pupils into mixed groups of girls and boys, with the shared task of observing whether boys actually talked more than girls in groups and what that meant for the individuals concerned. Through that activity, the teacher achieved 'a balanced exchange of views and some disclosure of personal attitudes'. Such strategies are sadly still unusual, rather than the norm.

Although patterns of educational disadvantage continue into the 1990s, there is evidence to suggest that girls and women are more able to challenge discrimination. The language of feminism has entered the vocabulary of young women, according to Riddell (1992). From her research study on girls in comprehensive schools in the south-west of England, conducted in the mid-1980s, she concluded that although the girls saw curriculum subjects in sex-differentiated terms, the picture today was very different from that which McRobbie had described in 1978. Boys and male teachers were described as sexist or 'male chauvinist pigs' and girls were critical of the ideology of romance. Di may have caught her prince – but the myth of 'happy ever after' has now been exploded.

Riddell argued that the female passivity suggested by some earlier researchers had disappeared and that girls' culture had changed. Girls were now more affected by external labour market considerations and by a wish to ensure a role for themselves in the labour market before taking on marriage and motherhood. These findings are very similar to research findings of my own, which are reported in some detail in Chapter 4.

But has the pattern of disadvantage shifted? Are young women today receiving chances and opportunities equivalent to their male peers? The answers to those questions are complex. Quantitative data – such as the analysis of pupil performance on GCSE from 1988 to 1990 – provides a picture of girls out-performing boys in examination attainment (reported by Stobart, Elwood and Quinlan, 1992).

In general, girls out-performed boys in subjects other than mathematics and some sciences. Between 1988 and 1990, 54.6 per cent of girls gained grades A–C in English, compared with 41.5 per cent of boys. The picture for mathematics was reversed, however, with 38.9 per cent of boys achieving a grade A–C, compared with 34.6 per cent of girls. In a number of those areas in which boys out-performed girls, such as biology, chemistry, economics and mathematics, the gap was slowly diminishing, whilst in areas in which girls out-performed boys, such as English literature, history, geography, French, the gap was increasing. Willms and Kerr (1988), looking at the educational trends in Scotland, reported a similar pattern.

The picture is very similar in the USA. More girls than boys now graduate from high school; there are more women than men on master's degrees and PhD programmes; and although fields of specialization remain there is also evidence to suggest that differences are disappearing (National Center for Educational Statistics, 1984; Hafner and Shaha, 1984).

So is gender inequality still an issue? Riddell (1992) reports that the publication in Scotland of these examination trends prompted an article from the *Times Educational Supplement, Scotland* (21.7.89) entitled, 'Advantage Girls' which argued that schools were now discriminating against boys and that boys' disadvantage should be an area for research. Perhaps this is a fair challenge:

> *If young women's achievements are so positive, why is gender still an issue for educators and researchers?*

I would suggest that there are three reasons for this continued focus:

- *The sustained impact of institutional sexism in schools.* Both the overt and the hidden curriculum still provide girls with an unequal educational experience.
- *The different areas of achievement.* Women are still excluded from many high-paying careers because they lag behind in science and mathematics.
- *The links between schooling, work and income.* Although women have largely closed the education attainment gap, they still receive far from equal rewards in their occupations.

SISTERS ACROSS THE OCEAN

In 1885 the American Association of University Women (AAUW) commissioned a national study to dispel the myth that higher education harmed women's health. Over a hundred years later, the same body commissioned *How Schools Shortchange Girls* (AAUW, 1992) to demonstrate that girls were still not receiving the same quality, or quantity, of education as their brothers.

The study summarized the findings of all the 35 major US task forces and commissions that had contributed to *A Nation at Risk* (US Department of Education, 1983), the major US governmental report which had set the tone and framework for educational reform in the USA to the year 2000. The researchers commissioned to carry out the study asked the following questions:

- To what degree had women participated as members, or held leadership positions, on the special task forces or commissions?
- Had the issues or concerns that prompted a particular report included gender or sex equity?
- Did the data, the rationale or the background information presented include sex, or gender, as a separate category?
- Had the recommendations specifically addressed gender issues?

The researchers reported a pattern of hidden discrimination in the way that government reports and commissions had conducted their activities. Women had been significantly under-represented in the 35 commissions, particularly in leadership positions; most of the reports had not defined the issues in terms of gender, had failed to analyse data or information in these terms, and had made few recommendations with gender in mind. The researchers concluded that reports from the task forces and commissions implied that 'the only significant problems girls may face are getting pregnant at an early age, dropping out of school and thereby increasing the number of female-headed households living in poverty' (ibid., p. 6).

The AAUW report argued that the lack of focus on gender both excluded girls from the national education goals set by *A Nation at Risk* and obscured the reality of the education experience of girls and young women. The report drew on a range of research to present a comprehensive analysis of how schools 'shortchanged girls' from the early years of education onwards.

It suggested that *pre-school education* 'shortchanged' girls by engaging them in activities in which they are already more proficient than boys. Girls therefore tended to achieve competency in the activities set by the schools and the schools turned their attention to boys. One consequence of this was that pre-school education experience reduced sex differences in language proficiency between girls and boys by raising boys' scores.

At *elementary school* activities targeted at encouraging boys' reading skills and girls' mathematical competencies reduced differences in performance between girls and boys. But as children become older the two critical issues become those of *opportunity* and *confidence*. Nine-year-old girls and boys expressed equal interest in science activities but girls were not given the opportunity to *do* as many activities. Tobin and Garnett (1987), for example, found that 79 per cent of demonstrations in mixed science classes were carried out by boys, which reduced girls' confidence and enthusiasm for science. The issue of confidence is important in influencing the choices which students make: whilst adolescent boys dropped maths and science because they lacked competence, girls dropped the subjects because they lacked confidence.

The AAUW report demonstrated how the high self-esteem which girls had about themselves was eroded by their educational experience in middle and junior schools. This *silencing* process has been described in the following terms:

> Young girls show striking capacities for self-confidence, courage and resistance to harmful norms of feminine behaviour, as well as a detailed and complex knowledge of the human social world . . . Up until the age of eleven or twelve . . . girls are quite clear and candid about what they think and feel and know.
>
> (Rogers and Gilligan, 1988, pp. 42–3)

But as girls reached mid-adolescence their voices became 'tentative and conflicted'. Classroom activities excluded girls, although with training and awareness teachers could tackle such inequalities. Secondary school classroom activities were also frequently organized as competitive ventures, rather than co-operative or collaborative exercises – a mode of working favoured more by boys than by girls and one that increased girls' alienation.

Sexual harassment was also part of the pattern of hidden discrimination which girls – although also occasionally boys – had to put up with. The AAUW report described how boys lined up to 'rate' girls as they entered a room, or embarrassed them to the point of tears. All too frequently, however, this was treated as a harmless joke by the school, an instance of 'boys being boys'.

Continuing on this theme, Shakeshaft (1992) has argued that schools are not safe places for females: that many school staff allow boys to rate girls on their anatomy and rarely challenge offensive sexist labelling, or name-calling. Girls are thus often taught in a 'hostile sexualized climate'. Shakeshaft suggested that the following incident represented the kinds of physical abuse which some young women suffered at school.

> A young woman who had been a cheerleader at our school received threatening notes and phone calls with sexual innuendoes, in school and at home. After football season was over, this young woman was told that, after track practice one day, that her mother had gotten into an accident near the school. The young woman, tricked into believing it was true, ran outside and was knocked out and assaulted, but not raped. The female student suffered terrible fear after the situation and missed a lot of school due to both physical and emotional reactions to this incident.
>
> (Bogart and Stein, 1987/89; quoted in Shakeshaft, 1992)

Shakeshaft concluded that female students experienced a high degree of sexual harassment from their peers and from staff. Her assertions were backed up by the findings from a study of allegations of sexual abuse and harassment of female students in 184 school districts in New York which showed that of the 300 reported incidents of harassment over a twelve-month period, 97 per cent of the staff abusers were heterosexual males and 74 per cent of their victims were female students (Shakeshaft and Cohan, 1990).

The picture in the USA is not dissimilar to that of the UK. It is a picture of girls achieving good examination results, despite the limitations of the educational process.

BLACK CHILDREN FAILING OR ACHIEVING?

This chapter has so far examined issues of class and gender in the schooling of girls. But issues of race are also integral to an understanding of girls' experience of schooling.

Government reports over the last 30 years about black children in schools have concentrated on explanations of, and remedies to tackle, their 'under-achievement'. The 1960s and 1970s saw three major policy shifts in government explanations for this apparent failure. In the early days of West Indian immigration to the UK, in the 1950s, the school under-achievement of black children was explained by their failure to assimilate into British society. It was assumed that once immigrant children had overcome cultural shock and developed their language skills, they would cease to be educationally disadvantaged (Bolton, 1979).

DES procedures for collecting statistics on immigrants, guided by the so-called 'ten-year' rule, were rooted in these assumptions. The 'ten-year' rule implied that after ten years in Britain, the children of immigrants would no longer face educational disadvantage attributable to their status as immigrants. The major education recommendations of this period were therfore for the provision of English as a second language and the development of cultural support systems for immigrant children. Despite the government recommendations for action, a major survey of local education authorities and schools in the early 1970s reported that the response of schools to the presence of immigrant children had been erratic and that an attitude of 'benign neglect' was prevalent in many local authorities (Townsend, 1971; Townsend and Brittan, 1972).

By the late 1960s and early 1970s, two major reports challenged the cultural assimilation policies. Both studies were based on the educational experience of children in the Inner London Education Authority (ILEA). The first report analysed ILEA pupils who had transferred from primary to secondary schools in September 1966. It showed that whilst the test scores of immigrant (West Indian) pupils improved markedly with increased length of schooling in this country, the test scores of black British children, born and educated in this country, were considerably below those of indigenous children (Little *et al.*, 1968).

The second report (Coard, 1971) reflected the views of the West Indian community and provided a powerful critique of the British education system. Coard argued that West Indian children were suffering grave injustices in the British education system. Coard's evidence drew on the experience of children in the ILEA, to show the disproportionate number of black children placed in educationally subnormal (ESN) schools: 16.9 per cent of the school population but 33.6 per cent of the population of ESN schools (1970 figures). Four out of five of the black children placed in ESN schools were West Indian.

Coard argued that West Indian children had been wrongly diagnosed as ESN because schools had rejected their language and culture; had failed to meet their linguistic needs; and had tested them inappropriately. Although Coard's work was later challenged, being described as a 'polemical pamphlet' (Taylor, 1981, p. 2), the DES also noted the disproportionately high numbers of black children placed in special schools (DES, 1971).

By 1973 the Select Committee on Race Relations had begun to acknowledge some of these issues and to make recommendations for local authority action:

> All local education authorities with sizeable immigrant child population should make plans to provide, by an early date, special facilities in ordinary schools to overcome the linguistic and adjustment problems of immigrant children with a level of ability higher than the general run of pupils in special schools for the educationally subnormal.
>
> (House of Commons, 1973)

Schools were urged to recognize and respond to the cultural and historical traditions of immigrants in order to facilitate their integration into British society. Although such thinking represented a shift in the educational policy (from assimilation to integration), the new integration model did little to challenge assumptions about the superiority of white Christian culture, or to recognize that racism was a constituent feature in black children's experience of British schooling (Bolton, 1979).

Such an acknowledgement was made, however, in 1977 with the publication of a Green Paper on education (DES, 1977). This argued that black culture, religions and languages would not diminish British culture, but broaden and enrich it: such an analysis represented a shift from integration to cultural pluralism. Once schools fully reflected the multiracial nature of society in their curriculum and practices, not only would the lives of schoolchildren be enriched but ignorance, prejudice and ultimately racism would be challenged.

The Green Paper had little impact, however, on schools – particularly those in areas with the lowest concentration of ethnic minority children (Riley, 1982). By the early 1980s, it had become clear that equality issues for black children had yet to reach the staffroom agenda.

> The educational problems confronting ethnic minority children have been extensively analysed from almost every conceivable angle. The outcome is unimpressive. Ethnic minority children and in particular West Indian pupils are still underachieving at school on a disturbing scale. Parents with high but not unrealistic aspirations for their children are still vocal in their dissatisfaction. Teachers recognize these symptoms and tend to lay responsibility at the door of the society and 'institutional racism'. Much of the research and advice of the last decade has been of little practical value, or at least has not been translated into suggestions capable of implementation. A decentralized system of education leaves each of the thousands of schools concerned having to find the best solutions the hard way. The teaching profession is defensive and fearful of being seen to treat one child different to another.
>
> (House of Commons, 1980–81, **I:** *Evidence*, para. 127)

RACISM IN SCHOOLS

Given the national assessment of discrimination and disadvantage, what was happening in the 1970s and early 1980s to black children (girls and boys) in the classroom? There was evidence to suggest that 'immigrant' children were consistently being placed in the lower streams of secondary schools (Townsend and Brittan, 1972; Troyna, 1978). Other research of the same period suggested that West Indian pupils were discouraged from taking O levels and were more likely to be entered for CSEs than their indigenous counterparts (Rex and Tomlinson, 1979; Rampton, 1981; Driver, 1980).

Classroom studies of the time attempted to provide explanations for these outcomes. Drawing on a participant observation study, Driver (1977) argued that the behaviour of teachers towards black pupils was often ambiguous. Teachers affected a 'colour-blind' stance towards pupils, yet consistently complained about the behaviour of West Indian pupils. The introduction of multicultural material had not necessarily increased teacher awareness of the impact of racism. In a later study he suggested that teachers encountered difficulties with West Indian pupils for a number of reasons. They consistently confused the names of West Indian pupils, well after they had learnt the names of the white pupils. They also held negative attitudes about West Indian language; were particularly threatened by the use of patois; and misunderstood many of the reflexive gestures, postures and signs used by West Indian pupils, thereby increasing the potential for conflict in the classroom (Driver, 1979).

A study (Mabey, 1980) carried out by ILEA's Research and Statistics Department found a similar picture. Mabey suggested that teachers often held negative perceptions of black children in a number of ways. They rated West Indian children as less likely to have good relations with their peers, less likely to have parents interested in their education and less likely to come from culturally stimulating homes. But how did the teachers themselves perceive these issues?

A study undertaken in ILEA schools in the mid-1970s suggested that many teachers were either blind to the implications of a multiracial school, or consciously opposed to them:

> A multiracial school is for many teachers often a euphemism for a racial and cultural mix of pupils from needy backgrounds. Hence less emphasis is placed on asking whether poverty is due to social injustice or to racial prejudice. The policy in many of these schools is to have teachers look and treat all children the same.
>
> (Giles, 1977, p. 74)

> I do not consider it the responsibility of an English state school to cater for the development of cultures and customs of a foreign nature.
>
> (Headteacher, ibid., p. 100)

There was growing evidence to suggest that such attitudes were contributing to the failure of black children. An overview of research studies on the educational performance of ethnic minority children in the 1970s suggested that the overwhelming research consensus was that black children were educationally disadvantaged (Tomlinson, 1980). Of the 33 studies Tomlinson considered, 26 of them found that ethnic minority children scored lower than white children on individual or group tests, were over-represented in ESN schools, or under-represented in higher streams of schools. Evidence included a longitudinal study based on data from the National Child Development Study which looked at 7,185 indigenous children and 1,045 immigrant children and concluded that when children were matched for similar social and home circumstances first-generation West Indian and Asian immigrants performed less well on attainment tests than indigenous children. Black British children (of both Asian and West Indian origin) had poorer test performance scores than indigenous children (Essen and Ghodsian, 1979).

A similar pattern of failure was found in the research analysis undertaken as background material for the Rampton Inquiry (1981) into the Education of Children from Ethnic Minority Groups (Taylor, 1981). Taylor was commissioned as part of the inquiry to evaluate 'important research evidence' on the educational performances of children of West Indian origin – a similar but much more detailed evaluation than that of Tomlinson. Taylor's analysis focused on the positivist tradition – large-scale investigations of the psychometric type – and excluded smaller ethnographic studies as being too descriptive.

Taylor provided Rampton with overwhelming evidence of under-achievement by pupils of West Indian origin. She concluded that on IQ, verbal and non-verbal, reading and mathematics tests, West Indian children performed more poorly than indigenous children and were also more likely to be found in the lower streams of ordinary schools and in higher proportions in ESN schools. The research evidence collated by Taylor, backed up other evidence presented to Rampton – for example from black parents' groups – contributed to the major conclusion of Rampton that racism, rather than language or 'adjustment problems', contributed significantly to the educational disadvantage of black children:

> We are convinced from the evidence we have obtained that racism both intentional and unintentional has a direct bearing on the performance of West Indian children in our schools.
>
> (Rampton, 1981, p. 12)

Rampton argued that the effect of this educational disadvantage was manifested in the relatively poor examination performance of West Indian pupils and their limited entry to further and higher education. DES figures presented to Rampton indicated that only 3 per cent of West Indian pupils achieved five O levels, compared with 16 per cent of other school leavers and 18 per cent of Asian school leavers. In higher education, only 1 per cent of West Indians undertook degree courses, compared with 4 per cent of other students and 5 per cent of Asian students. West Indian pupils were more likely to be taking lower-level non-advanced further education courses than other students: 15 per cent of West Indian pupils took FE courses compared with 7 per cent of other students and 11 per cent of Asian students (Rampton, 1981, pp. 6–9).

Although the picture presented by Rampton was one of blanket discrimination, disadvantage and disillusionment with the school system, the situation was more complex than this. Children of West Indian origin were less likely to be absent from schools than indigenous children. Davies (1981), for example, found that the absence rate for black children in three secondary schools was 10 per cent, compared with an absence rate of 20 per cent for white children. One explanation put forward for this was that black pupils and parents attached greater importance to schooling than white pupils and parents.

Davies also found that although the average absence rate for girls and boys overall was similar, girls in the single-sex school in her study had a much lower absence rate than girls in the coeducational school. Davies's study did not, unfortunately, compare the attendance of black girls and black boys, nor did it account for the differences in attendance between girls in the single-sex and coeducational schools. In the way that much of the research on gender has obscured issues of race and class, so much of the work on race has obscured issues of class and gender.

UNDER-ACHIEVEMENT: A COMPLEX PATTERN

A few research studies in the 1980s challenged this consensus of blanket failure from black children, suggesting that at O level or CSE the academic performance of West Indian pupils was equal to, or better than, that of white children in urban schools. The researchers identified issues of class and gender as being critical to an understanding of the achievement of black students.

Bagley, for example, argued that blanket statements about the under-achievement of black children were untenable. Black children were more likely than white to attend schools with a high teacher turnover and high pupil absenteeism. Pupils in those schools were also more likely to be socially disadvantaged than pupils in other schools (Bagley, 1975; Bagley, Mallick and Verma , 1979). Teachers also tended to assume that black British children were uniformly working class and disadvantaged (Giles, 1977). Bagley also suggested that teachers were unable to distinguish class differences amongst black children and assumed a uniformity of cultural and educational experiences for all black children and their parents.

Bagley argued that the most academically successful children were those who had originated from parts of the Caribbean other than Jamaica (in particular Trinidad, Barbados and Guyana); whose parents were well educated and high achievers, who spoke Creole and standard English; and were most critical of the English education system. He suggested, like Foner (1978), that many immigrant Jamaican parents had originated from rural areas and had received few educational opportunities in Jamaica. Nevertheless, they placed great value on education although they were not in a position to criticize the schooling offered to their children in England (Bagley, ibid.).

Similarly, Driver (1978, 1980) argued that on overall achievement (public examinations at 16), specific performance in those examinations in English, mathematics and science, and general persistence in school work, West Indian pupils excelled over indigenous pupils, and West Indian girls were the most successful overall. He also suggested that in some schools, but not in others, black female pupils were academically successful.[4]

Fuller (1980) also concluded that West Indian girls performed better in external examinations than indigenous girls, black boys or white boys and were second in achievement only to Asian boys. She accounted for these differences by suggesting that the black girls formed a discernible subculture wihin the school which was based on a strong sense that they had of their own self-worth and a clear view that they could help take control of their own lives through academic success. Fuller, along with later writers (Riley, 1985a, b; Mac an Ghaill, 1988; Reid, 1989) found a subculture of activity, creativity and resistance.

RESISTANCE OR DISCRIMINATION?

As a London secondary school teacher in the 1970s, I began to puzzle about the interconnections between class, race and gender and the contradiction between what research had to say about young black women and my own teaching experience. Both national research and research from the ILEA suggested a pattern of under-achievement for black children. Ten years of teaching in inner London schools had led me to believe that in some schools black girls were succeeding.

I became very keen to explore what contributed to the success or failure of both young black and white women in different schools. I was puzzled by the way both researchers and administrators couched the debate about school success or failure. The word 'quality' had yet to enter into the educationalists' lexicon and success and failure were largely measured by O levels and CSEs. But how did policy-makers know whether a school was succeeding for its pupils, or failing them?

Three significant reports reinforced an initial decision I had made to explore these issues. The first was *Fifteen Thousand Hours* (Rutter *et al.*, 1979), a study in school effectiveness which argued that schools could indeed affect the behaviour and attainment of pupils and have a positive influence on both their development and on education outcomes. The analysis from the Rutter research showed that schools with similar resources and similar pupil intakes could produce different outcomes for students.

My interest in the Rutter study was heightened by the experience of having been a teacher in one of the schools in the study. As a relatively new teacher to London and a newly appointed deputy head of year, I had been interviewed by Peter Mortimore, then one of the researchers and now Professor at the Institute of Education, London.

Regrettably, the findings of the Rutter study were never fed directly back to us and I recall spending one or two anxious moments with other staff searching to see where we came in the tables at the back of the book. Nevertheless, the research had a profound effect on me. It signalled to me that the individual efforts and activities of teachers in classrooms did matter and that joint efforts to plan for improvement and to develop the positive ethos of a school could enrich children's lives. It made the struggle of inner-city teaching seem worthwhile.

The study also caused me to ask some broader questions about the overall performance of the school I was teaching in. How did we fare compared with neighbouring schools? As we struggled to keep afloat, did we end up suspending more children than other schools? But it also left me with another question, not satisfactorily answered by Rutter: Were we more successful with some groups of children than others?

Two other reports reinforced my desire to explore what was happening in schools: the Scarman Report on the Brixton disorders in 1981, and the Rampton Report on the educational performance of black children. The influence of the Scarman Report included the impact of the riots themselves. Living and working as I then did in south London, it was impossible to have been unaffected by the riots or to have seen them in quite the terms described by the media (Riley, 1982). The riots had been about racism, disaffection and anger – a community turning on to itself. I have no wish to glorify them, but they did demonstrate energy, involvement and a desire to take control of the local area. The conflicting feelings of the local community about the events were shared by the pupils that I taught.

The Brixton riots enabled some of the racism issues that had been bubbling under the surface for many years to emerge. Many of these issues were reflected in the Scarman Report, and later in the Rampton Report. The significance of the Rampton Report was that it was the first time that an official education document had acknowledged the impact of racism in schools.

In writing some years ago on the Brixton disorders and the Scarman Report, I introduced an article with the following two accounts.

Incident 1

Date: February 1981

Scene: a large multiracial school in Brixton.

Action: M, a former black pupil, revisits the school to keep an appointment with a member of staff. A senior teacher, who is new to the school and therefore unaware that he is talking to a former pupil, calls the police because, as he put it later, the boy did not show 'due deference'.

When the police arrived, M was in the tuckshop in the company of the member of staff with whom he had the appointment. He was pulled out of the shop and pinned to the ground by several policemen. At one point there were thirteen policemen in the school playground. This all took place in front of young, impressionable pupils waiting to buy goods from the tuckshop.

(This account is taken from evidence to the Scarman Inquiry.)

Incident 2

Date: November 1981

Scene: a teacher training institute in the home counties.

Action: A fourth-year BEd student says to a sociology lecturer: 'I very much enjoyed the book you lent me on black women in Britain. There is just one thing I am worried about. Are Asian women the ones with straight hair or with crinkly hair?'

I then suggested that the issue raised by the two incidents was not whether racism existed in schools but who brought it through the school gates. The question for the 1990s is: could similar events take place today? It is obviously difficult to answer such a question simply. Certainly, the MacDonald Report on the murder of a student at Burnage School reported racism and also the limitations of anti-racist policies (MacDonald *et al.*, 1989). It is perhaps also worth reflecting that Chapter 2 raised the concern from officers in a number of local authorities that the capacity of local authorities to tackle racism had been weakened by aspects of the Education Reform Act (Taylor, 1992).

The sort of questions in my mind in the late 1970s were: Is the experience of racism the same for black girls and boys? How do white girls and boys perceive racism? What have class and gender to do with all this? Underpinning these questions was a belief that if schools were to effect change for all their pupils, they needed to understand what was happening to groups of pupils. Turning a 'gender-' or 'colour-blind' eye merely compounded the disadvantage.

My research agenda was also influenced by the tendency of research studies about schools to focus on males (usually white). The invisibility of young women was a constant annoyance. I also read studies about the alienation of black youth and their identification with black Rastafarian subculture. Garrison (1979), for example, argued that young black women were mere appendages to this black male culture. But this did not accord with my experience. The young black women I taught made it clear to me that they were not peripheral to a dominant male youth culture, but had a definable set of attitudes and culture that were very much their own. They were determined to challenge many aspects of sex stereotyping.

I wanted to examine how young black and white women – other than those I taught – experienced schooling, and to examine whether stereotypes of female passivity existed. In particular, I wanted to examine how those young women equipped themselves for the future. Many of the young black women I had taught had been successful academically and had shown a great determination to build up qualifications for the future – but would they be equipped to deal with both racial and sexual disadvantage in the labour market? What were schools doing to equip them?

Chapter 4 is an account of my research and some follow-up work.

NOTES

1. Research on class (such as that of Floud, Halsey and Martin, 1956; and more recently McPherson and Raab, 1988) has largely ignored issues of gender and ethnicity. Feminist analysis has only just begun to tackle the inter-relationship between the three (Anthias and Yuval Davis, 1983; Safia Mirza, 1992). According to Foner (1978), research on racial disadvantage has failed to take into account differences in occupational background. Similarly, educational research on special needs has seen this group of children as singularly unaffected by issues of race, gender and class.
2. Dyhouse (1981) has suggested that such developments were linked to fears about the future of the British race and the decline of the Empire as Britain faced both military and industrial challenges from Germany and Japan.

3. As was discussed in Chapter 2, the three types of schools to be set up in the tripartite system were grammar schools, technical schools and modern schools. Very few technical schools were opened.

4. Critics have suggested that Driver sensationalized his findings in an article in *New Society*, 17 January 1980 (Carrington, 1981).

Chapter 4

Black and white girls – yesterday and today

> But people might think we're greedy just wanting equal rights. But it shouldn't be greedy but it should be how the world should be.
>
> (Girl at Marchbank School, 1993)

INTRODUCTION

This chapter draws on some of the findings from an extensive research study which I carried out in 1980–81 in three schools, two single-sex and one coeducational (Riley, 1985a), and a follow-up in one coeducational school in 1993. The timespan between the two pieces of work covers three Conservative administrations, which allows some reflections to be made on the impact of radical Conservatism on the lives of the young women.

The original research focused on the pupils' experience of schooling; their expectations for the future, particularly in relation to the labour market; and parental expectations. The analysis presented in this chapter focuses on the first element of the research – pupils' experience of schooling – in an attempt to illuminate some of the themes and issues raised in Chapter 3. In particular:

- the quality of the education experience available for young people (especially in inner-city areas);
- how issues of race, gender and class impact on that experience;
- the scope that teachers and schools have to influence that experience; and
- how these experiences have changed over the last decade.

The investigation had as its background various research and government reports projecting an overwhelming consensus about the educational failure of black children (a consensus that some studies challenged; see Chapter 3). What the research found was a complex pattern of widely differing school experiences and achievement among the students being investigated. Black and white girls in the two single-sex schools had a qualitatively different educational experience as compared with girls in the coeducational school. Another finding was that significant differences existed in how schools approached issues of race and that turning a 'colour-blind eye' to the presence of black children – as happened in one school – had the effect of increasing their disadvantage.

The study also found differences in academic achievement: between black and white girls in one school; between black girls and boys; and between groups of black girls. Some young black women – notably those from parts of the Caribbean other than Jamaica – were academically successful compared with their white counterparts – a finding which could be related to class experiences and expectations.

THE RESEARCH

The original research was based in three schools in south London: one coeducational comprehensive (Greenvale); one single-sex, voluntary aided grammar (Christchurch); and one single-sex comprehensive (Crossland). All three schools served largely inner-city populations, although Greenvale was located in relatively leafy suburban surroundings. Two hundred and six fifth-year (Year 11) girls and 49 boys completed questionnaires and of this group 74 girls and 49 boys were interviewed. In completing the questionnaire, pupils were asked to indicate their parental origins and to categorize themselves, for example, as British, Black-British, Afro-Caribbean. The bulk of the respondents fell into two broad categories: A – parental origin English, Scottish or Irish; and B – parental origin Afro-Caribbean (see Table 4.1).

Table 4.1 Ethnic origin of pupils

	No. of pupils who completed the questionnaire			No. of pupils who were interviewed		
	A	B	C	A	B	C
Female pupils						
Greenvale	26	11	3	8	9	1
Crossland	32	53	15	8	25	4
Christchurch	43	8	15	8	8	3
Total	101	72	33	24	42	8
Male pupils						
Greenvale	21	22	6	9	9	1

Source: Riley (1985a)

The analysis presented in this chapter focuses on the experiences of those two groups of children. Pupils of mixed-race parentage were categorized on the basis of their black parent, on the assumption that such students would be perceived as black in our society, and that attitudes and expectations towards them would be based on this perception. The research sample also included children from a range of countries whose family origins included Cyprus, Greece, India and France. This grouping is described as category C in Table 4.1 but is not included in the analysis in this chapter.[1]

Before beginning the research, I had reflected on the limitations of myself as researcher: a white woman whose education had moved her into the middle classes. Ultimately, I took the view that, as a researcher and educationalist, I had to take some responsibility for issues of gender, race and class. Whilst I think my interviews with black and white girls were fruitful, those with black and white boys were singularly unilluminating. Issues of race and gender have complex and differing consequences.

The research dealt with a complex web of inter-related factors:

- *gender issues:* an exploration of any differences between the educational experience for girls in the two single-sexed schools compared with girls in the mixed school;
- *race issues:* the degree to which the three schools perceived and tackled racism and how race issues emerged for pupils; and
- *class issues:* the nature of the curriculum; and teacher expectations and assumptions about pupils.

The research findings demonstrated the importance of unpacking issues of race, class and gender: an exercise that remains equally relevant today. Such an approach enables a clearer understanding of the range of factors which influence the process and outcomes of schooling. It helps to identify instances where schools may be successful for some groups of pupils but not for others. Most importantly, such a detailed analysis of equality dimensions enables schools and local authorities to develop strategies which will improve the quality of experience for all pupils. It also provides a basis for their accountability to parents. The research findings are outlined to demonstrate how such an analysis can inform our understanding of failure and success in schools and what can be gained from talking to pupils.

GENDER

Whilst I was undertaking the fieldwork for the research, I was also teaching in a single-sex girls' comprehensive school, Lavender Hill in Battersea. As I moved from Lavender Hill to the coeducational school Greenvale, I was struck daily by the difference between Greenvale and my own school, as well as the differences between Greenvale, and Christchurch and Crossland. At Lavender Hill, I had been used to young women who were lively, very visible around the school and occasionally very loud-mouthed! Walking into Greenvale at any recreational period, I had to search hard to find the girls. They were hidden in the cloakrooms, on the periphery of the play areas and in the corners of halls and dining-rooms.

Life at Greenvale: 'girls'' subjects and 'boys'' subjects

Greenvale adopted a 'gender-blind' approach to its pupils, and by so doing subsumed the needs and interests of its female pupils to those of its male pupils. At Greenvale, the school's hidden curriculum, through the provision of leisure facilities, the school hierarchy and discipline practices, reproduced patterns of male domination. As part of this culture of male domination, the school's institutionalized counselling practices, used at various key points in pupils' school careers to guide their choices of subjects and future careers, effectively deflected and 'cooled' out female participation in designated 'male' areas of the curriculum, or the labour market.

I have described the process which delineated the curriculum choice of girls and boys as the 'choice mechanism'. The concept owes much to an American study (Cicourel and Kitsuse, 1963) that demonstrated how the counselling system in a high school incorporated a 'cooling-out' process which deflected the 'overhigh' ambitions of working-class and black students.

Greenvale's 'choice mechanism' first came into effect at the end of pupils' second year at the school when they were offered the choice, for the third year, of three periods either of home economics or of technical drawing. Male pupils had to inform the male head of Design & Technology of their choice; female pupils, the female head of Home Economics. (Home economics was not a separate department, but a subsidiary department of the Design & Technology Department.)

The school's 'choice mechanism' was perpetuated through the counselling process for 4th- and 5th-year option choices. Although the option sheet presented to 3rd-year pupils stated that all subjects were open to both boys and girls, this choice did not exist in practice. Girls were counselled by female heads of house who were resistant to change and discouraged girls from participating in non-traditional school subjects. The head of Design & Technology suggested that housemistresses counselled girls against technical drawing, as he believed the limited number of places in technical drawing for 4th-year pupils could be best used by boys. Thus Greenvale's options counselling system, far from redressing gender inequalities – few Greenvale girls had experienced craft and technology in the third year – reinforced institutionalized sexism within the school.

In the 4th year, the 'choice mechanism' was reinforced by structural timetabling arrangements. Greenvale required those pupils who studied metalwork or woodwork also to take technical drawing. This inflexible requirement was a particular disincentive to female pupils:

> I did it in the third year – woodwork and metalwork. I did it for one year. It was a new thing when I came into the third year. I didn't like needlework at the time; I enjoyed cooking. So me and my friend were the only two girls in the class, the rest were boys. I enjoyed woodwork, but not metalwork. They said you can choose it as an option, but I liked cooking, although I didn't like needlework, but I chose cooking instead ... You couldn't do woodwork, cookery, nothing like that. It had to be woodwork and metalwork. It would have been good if I could have done cooking and woodwork.
>
> (Caron, a white girl)

The effect of the school's hidden curriculum, and specifically its 'choice mechanism' was that by the time female pupils in the study had reached their 5th year, none took design & technology – one girl had chosen the subject in the 4th year, but ultimately had withdrawn from the course – and only two girls took physics. Few girls at Greenvale had been willing to combat the stereotypes. One of the girls taking physics described her experience in the following terms:

In my physics class, there's only me and this other girl [Karen]: that's the only girls in our class. It's hard ... Bit embarrassing sometimes, like when you've gotta do experiments, you've got to do it with the boys ... A lot of girls do biology, but not physics, I don't know why ... When they [other pupils] found out about the boys ... they said I'd picked physics 'cos I wanted to go with the boys.

(Yvonne, a black girl)

Yvonne later explained that she had been encouraged by her father, a science teacher, to take physics, but that without the presence and support of the other girl in the group, Karen, she probably would not have continued the course. More typically, given the pressures, girls chose a conventional range of subjects.

The girls are encouraged more on cookery than anything else you know. You never see hardly any girls doing TD or anything like that ... Yeah, they can do it, it's up to them. But you see with girls you can get the teachers saying that ain't a girls' subject, and things like that ... You know most of them give a funny look sort of, if you're doing TD and there's a whole group of boys there and you've got funny looks from teachers saying, 'Mmm?' right, and the girls don't think, well, don't think that it's a kind of girls' subject in a way. It's been put on as a boys' subject ... and cookery as a girls' subject.

(Margaret, a white girl)

The 'choice mechanism' at Greenvale was reinforced in a complex way by the careers information provided by the male head of careers. School career events focused on 'male occupations from which girls were categorically excluded. The school's organizational arrangements also consistently excluded girls.

The people that come in for careers, it's all for boys, which I think is unfair. I don't see why they can't get nurses coming in; secretaries; doctors; social workers. People to come in and tell you about the jobs they do. You get the Army and the Navy coming in for the boys, with demonstrations and lectures; you don't get anything for the girls.

There's nothing offered for the girls at lunch time, apart from if you've got to practise. But the boys, they get football, they get table-tennis, things that keep them out of trouble, but they've got nothing to keep girls out of trouble, so you just see them walking around or sitting down chattering ...

I'd like to play table-tennis, but I can't get anybody to play with me. If you want to play when the boys come down to play, they just run in, grab a table ... They said the girls could play table-tennis if they wanted to, all they've got to do is go to Mr X [deputy headteacher] and say, 'We wanna play table-tennis', and he'll go and say to the boys, 'Get off the table, we want the girls to play.' But you know it's rather wicked – they should set aside tables for the girls so you can play.

(Karen, a black girl)

The hidden curriculum at Greenvale systematically reinforced male power relations. There were no organizational steps to challenge this, and indeed the institutional practices embedded within the subject 'choice mechanism' operated as a powerful deterrent to those young women who wanted to challenge power relations. The 'gender contradictions' expressed by the majority of the girls at Greenvale were both an inevitable response to the pressure and conflicts which they faced daily and also an indication of their resistance. The achievement of the young women was that many of them – particularly the young black women – were able to put forward some views that were in conflict with the ethos of the school.

Crossland and Christchurch

The daily lives of the girls in the two single-sex schools, Crossland and Christchurch, were considerably different from those of girls at Greenvale. At both schools, the message given was 'Girls are important.' Assemblies at both schools, usually conducted by female members of staff, reinforced this message.

Both schools offered a wide range of recreational activities for their pupils. Girls at Crossland and Christchurch were clearly visible at lunch breaks, in marked comparison with their peers at Greenvale. At Crossland the main playground activities were football and netball. Gymnastics was also popular as a physical pursuit, and typing, a sedentary but equally popular lunch-time activity. Another important recreational pursuit was photography, with much of the girls' work displayed around the school. Also on display were photographs recording a number of school-organized plays, dance shows and activity holidays, such as skiing.

The recreational activities offered at Christchurch were different from those at Crossland. They were more structured, more tightly supervised and linked to the Christian ethos of the school. During Lent, for example, many pupils undertook to raise money for various charities. Break and lunch-time activities included sales of food made by the pupils' sponsored games and other such fund-raising activities. In addition, Christchurch offered sporting activities such as netball.

At Crossland, both black and white girls complained about the restricted subject choice and argued that the curriculum offered to them reflected traditional thinking of what girls and women should do. They wanted a broader curriculum, which would allow them to choose 'male' and 'female' subjects: cookery *and* woodwork. Black girls, in particular, emphasized the need to choose adventurously in science and technology fields. They argued that their future career prospects were being blighted by the limitations of the curriculum offered to them. Several also argued that the curriculum failed to provide them with the opportunities to gain skills which would enable them to be both economically and domestically independent: 'Like painting and decorating. If I can get me own flat, I can do it myself' (Patricia, a black girl).

Out of the 25 black girls interviewed at Crossland 20 were critical of the restricted subject choice, and complained about the school's bias to 'girls' stuff'. They mentioned physics, technology, metalwork, woodwork, additional mathematics, technical drawing, plastics, computers, motor and car mechanics and engineering. Woodwork was a particular favourite, and was mentioned by the majority of black girls:

Q   What subjects would you bring in to the school?

A   I'd bring things like physics ... there was SC1Z, which is a combination of all three sciences, but not enough of us chose it, so they crossed it off ... And I would offer things like technical drawing, 'cos some girls are interested in that. I want to do computers.

(Kay, a black girl)

The white girls also complained about the over-emphasis in the curriculum on the domestic role of women: 'You're not always gonna get married. Some people are gonna live on their own' (Christine, a white girl). At Christchurch there were distinct differences in the views of the black and white girls about the curriculum. All eight of the black girls interviewed argued that the academic curriculum offered by the school failed to meet the needs of the changing world. They argued for a radically different curriculum that would be based more in sciences, technology and business and suggested that the school should offer woodwork, metalwork, engineering, technical drawing, a wider range of sciences, business studies and typing. As at Crossland, woodwork was a favourite, not for O level, but 'just for fun'.

Woodwork – I think we should be able to do those things. The world's changing. Engineering, woodwork and things like that. Just for fun, to see what it is like. [Schools should] think more about the outside world. Like geography doesn't really teach you very much. When you get outside, you're not going to learn much. More to do with business, science and engineering, and woodwork – that sort of thing.

(Wendy, a black girl)

In contrast, only 2 of the 8 white girls interviewed would have liked to have had the opportunity to have experienced a broader range of subjects. A further 3 suggested, however, that the school should have offered a broader choice, but within the same academic framework. The white girls' endorsement of the curriculum offered at Christchurch is summed up by Stacey:

One of my friends wanted to be an engineer ... I don't think people [at school] think it's a good idea ... I don't think it's very good for a girl to try. It's great if you're a success, but not if you're not! Men just don't seem to be able to take an interest in women doing that sort of job. I know it's stupid ... very sexist, but that's how it is.

(Stacey, a white girl)

At Crossland and Christchurch the limitations on the educational experience offered to girls were imposed by the overt rather than the hidden curriculum: a traditional girls' secondary modern curriculum at Crossland and a traditionally girls' grammar school curriculum at Christchurch. Although Greenvale did not officially distinguish between the curriculum offered to either sex, in reality it offered a very sex-differentiated curriculum. It was a mixed school that girls happened to attend.

A consequence of these differing experiences was that girls at both Crossland and Christchurch were more likely to state their willingness to participate in curriculum areas that have been seen as traditionally male and more likely to assert their willingness to participate on equal terms with males in the labour market, than girls at Greenvale.

RACE AND RACISM

How issues of race and gender were experienced by both black and white girls in the three schools depended less on whether they had attended a single-sex or coeducational school and more on the attitude of the school to race and the proportion of black pupils attending the school.

Greenvale and Crossland

At Greenvale and Crossland both black and white girls acknowledged that the black girls were an important part of the school population. This recognition stemmed from the physical presence of black girls in the school (28 per cent of the female 5th-year group at Greenvale and 53 per cent at Crossland), but also from the school climate. In both schools the young black women felt that they could assert themselves as young, female and black despite the existence of racism:

> Some people are prejudiced against the pupils in this school. It's okay in this school, because there's equal blacks and whites, but if there was only a few black people, we'd be really run down bad. ·
>
> (A black girl, Greenvale)

> My friend goes to K school. I think it's more racialist up there. There's more white kids. But here it's mixed ... you don't see racialist writing around everything.
>
> (A black girl, Crossland)

In both Crossland and Greenvale there was little articulated racism from the white girls but a positive assertion that the presence of black pupils and the determined efforts by the schools themselves to reflect the interests of the black students and inform white students about racism had been beneficial.

> There's all different colours and they [teachers] treat everyone the same, and that's what I like about this school ... You can get really nice coloured people. I've got a lot of coloured friends. You can get bad whites

as well . . . They mix well, that's another thing that I like about it . . . [My friends] . . . a black girl, a white girl . . . about five white girls and three blacks in a group.

(Caron, a white girl, Greenvale)

I mean you get really nice coloured people. You get nice people really at this school . . . I'm mates with a coloured girl . . . We was watching this film in school and this coloured man went into a pub and it says 'No coloured people allowed', you know, and there was all white people. I think it was called *In the Heat of the Night* – good film.

(Donna, a white girl, Crossland)

There was also a view, however, that an underlying tension existed between black and white girls at extreme moments of conflict:

Black girls go round with a white girl, where the white girl's more or less like the same as a black girl – sort of like the same things. I know quite a lot of black girls go around with white girls. I mean I'll go with white girls if they're sort of like me . . . I don't think colour matters, but I suppose if there's going to be a fight between a black girl and a white girl, all the black girls gather round and the white girls would think that all the black girls was gonna join in. Sometimes they do. But I know that black people have got tempers, or they seem to have more than white people.

(Ivy, a black girl, Greenvale)

The minority of white girls who held overtly racist views had been challenged in their views by the school. In the following extract, Sally, a white girl from Greenvale, articulated the racist views held by members of her family. These views, however, had been clearly challenged by the school and had caused Sally to reflect on her own racism. The extract is a good example of how an individual teacher, or school, can use its influence to tackle racism.

My mates go to X [local Catholic school] and they say it's spot the white people in your school; I go 'No.' There's loads of people prejudiced here. My mates are. Victoria, she likes 'em to a certain extent. I say to her, 'Colour doesn't matter.' She said to me, 'If I catch you going out with a coloured boy, I'll kill you.' I said, 'I wouldn't go out with a nigger anyway, not 'cos of their colour, but I know my dad'd kill me. My dad, he ain't National Front . . . My Uncle Mickey though, he's terrible . . . this boy, he came and asked my Uncle Mickey – he was drunk anyway, and he came and asked him the time, and he goes: 'Don't ask me, you black c____' Oh, he's bad, he hates 'em. Maybe some of it wore off on my dad . . . I've got white friends and black friends . . . I go round with black people.

Some coloured people come up to you and say, 'You white bitch', and just turn round and say, 'You black nigger.' Like my English teacher's all for ... I've forgotten his name. Blair Peach. There was this girl came into our English class and this boy, he was a Paki ... and she said, 'Bloody Paki', and Miss C sent her out of the room. I mean everyone mucks about calling people Pakis ... She sent her to the Housemistress ... I don't like or dislike them, I just say 'Hello', and that's it ... Well you can't call them wogs can you? I dunno. Everyone goes, 'A pint of curry and a glass of water, keeps me going for an hour and a quarter.' ... I don't know because they eat curry.

Teachers – they're not allowed in this school, if they're prejudiced, because it's mixed. Jobs – if I went for an interview and there was a coloured girl, and just the two of you, and they said, 'I'm going to give you the job, 'cos she's a wog,' I'd feel awful horrible. I'd just say, because she's coloured, and you're not giving her the job, you can stick your old job.

(Sally, a white girl, Greenvale)

Christchurch

The experience of being a black student was considerably different for black girls at Christchurch. Although they shared with their black peers at Greenvale and Crossland a strong sense of identity as a group, they were also isolated and defensive. At both Crossland and Greenvale, the black girls had commented positively on being part of the school population:

Here it's mixed, it's just like one big happy family.

(Sharon, a black girl, Crossland)

There's equal black and white here.

(Yvonne, a black girl, Greenvale)

A contrasting comment from a Christchurch student was:

Well, you don't get much chance in this school because there's not many black people here, anyway.

(Naomi, a black girl)

All 8 of the black girls interviewed at Christchurch argued that colour was important for them. But their sense of identity was both limited and apologetic and based on a need to 'stick to one colour ... stick together ... go around together', rather than any positive assertion of themselves as young black women. For many of them there was a degree of ambivalence: a tension between their need to 'stick together' as a black group, and a view that they 'got on' with their white peers. Their need to 'stick together' extended throughout their school lives, and not just at times of conflict, as it had for the black girls at Crossland and Greenvale:

I get on with everybody in my class. Like you get some blacks and they like white music, and pop, and things like that, and some get so they just like reggae and they stick to one colour. It doesn't bother me at all, I just stick to what I believe, rather than follow someone else . . . All the blacks, we go round together . . . but we get on with everybody in the class. Sometimes, when we go home, we go with different people, because we all live in different areas, but we tend to stick together. But we get on with everybody, even if we're in class and we're joking and we call each other names, we know that we don't mean it . . . We all go around together . . . I suppose it's like their beliefs, or sometimes, if they go out to a club where they're playing reggae and they stick together.

(Sharon, a black girl)

The black girls at Christchurch had to cope with the ignorance of the white girls about them, and had to struggle to have their existence acknowledged as young black women. Out of the 8 young black women interviewed 7 argued that either they had personally experienced racism, or had observed racism, either from pupils or teachers, directed towards other black pupils.

Sometimes they [white girls] ask some silly questions. Because we're black, we're different. I know we're different, but there are certain things both black and white people do . . . We have to put grease on our hair, and they think that's silly. This girl asked me, 'How do you curl your hair?' and I said, 'Curlers, what do you think?' I think she thought we used bones or something . . . We did have an argument, but it was a friendly one. We were saying, if there weren't black people, there'd be nobody to drive the buses and things like that . . . Most of my friends are coloured or mixed, but I get on well with white people.

(Wendy, a black girl)

They also argued, as did their black peers from the other schools, that colour polarized opinions at times of conflict in the school. However, for the Christchurch girls, their presence as a black minority group made them vulnerable to racism:

[Colour matters] only when you have arguments. They bring it out, I found that. I've got nothing against them, I don't bring it out, only if they do sometimes. I just get angry, but you should just ignore them. [I go round with] black people. I used to go with white people, but we had a lot of arguments. Everybody has arguments in our class, but then we got singled out (swearing, like – I can't say 'Black bastard' and that kind of thing). The group I'm with now, I think they've always been together, but there's one Greek with us, but mostly mixed. When I was at my last school, there was only about two black people . . . [I go round with black girls] . . . Probably, to do with their lifestyles: they've got more in common. Really, I'd like to go round with people who live near me, but there's none: they're all too far away.

(Claudette, a black girl)

The views of the white girls at Christchurch were very different from those from the other two schools. All of the white girls argued that black girls made colour matter. They resented any manifestation of group solidarity by the black girls, and talked of 'we' whites and 'them' blacks. None of the white girls thought that there was any racial discrimination in the school and none talked, as some of the white girls had at the other two schools, of the positive advantages of having black girls in the school. They held stereotypes about black people who had a 'chip on their shoulder'.

> I think even though the blacks won't admit it, they've got a chip on their shoulder, and they won't accept a white girl ... If a person's black and she's got a chip on her shoulder, she's gonna go out of her way to get in the teacher's bad books ... A lot of it stems from colour. We accept blacks, but when we have a joke about a black person, we feel awkward about it.
> Blacks go around with blacks and whites, but they get on with each other. Black girls are bitchy, they don't like talking to black boys ... There's not many blacks in our school and everyone gets on with everyone ... There were big arguments between blacks and whites after the Brixton riots.
>
> (Colette, a white girl)

The isolation of the black girls at Christchurch was evident in the perceptions that the white girls had about them.

> There's only about seven black kids: they're all right. You sort of muck about with their hair, they don't take offence.
>
> (Vivian, a white girl)

> I don't think colour matters ... Everyone's the same ... Everyone's treated the same ... It really gets on my nerves, because everyone's meant to be the same ... If somebody says something, immediately everything's brought up as a racial problem ... Well, most of the time, it's the blacks, you know, it's the coloured girls that do it ... Coloured girls all in one group. I can't see any problem why they shouldn't think the same ... We were talking about how white people are different from black, and it got a bit fraught. Afterwards everyone laughed it off.
>
> (Alex, a white girl)

Christchurch was located in an area which was known for a high degree of white working-class racism. But the school made no overt challenge to racism and adopted a 'colour-blind' approach as its policy. Several of the black girls commented, for example, that issues such as race and racism had never been discussed in the classroom. It was this invisibility which served to undermine the confidence of the young black women. The school's failure to address racism exposed pupils such as

Claudette to racist name-calling and meant that the racially stereotyped views which a number of white pupils held had never been challenged.

RACE AND GENDER: THE DYNAMICS AT GREENVALE

As Greenvale was a coeducational school, the issues of race and gender impacted on the daily lives of pupils in particular ways. Forty-five per cent of the 5th-year boys and 28 per cent of the girls at Greenvale were black and both the processes and outcomes of schooling were different for black girls and boys. As a group, the black girls differentiated their behaviour and attitudes to school from their black male peers. Although peer group interaction was as important for the girls as the boys, the black girls, unlike the boys, did not perceive themselves as being in a state of continual conflict with their white peers. Black girls described the experience and behaviour of black boys in the school in the following terms:

> They act too childish, you know; they don't act sensible, as if they're grown up or anything. To me, I think they've got nothing in their heads ... A while back, you used to find the white boys fighting the coloured boys, and they all used to gang up on each other and that which I thought was stupid. 'Cos like say, a white boy's telling against the boy is a black nigger, and the coloured boy will go up and fight him, and then the whole lot of them will join in, and start beating up this one boy, which is childish 'cos all they have to do is just take it and walk off, but they didn't ... The white girls and the coloured girls in this school, we all get on good, you know. But it's the boys, we find them very funny against each other ...
>
> Some of them, all they're interested in is dressing nicely, having nice girls, a place that's all, and having good music and having fun. That's all they're interested in, some of them. And then another lot of them want a good career, the rest of them don't ... Girls are more determined ... 'cos my mum encourages me more than my brother.
>
> (Marion, a black girl)

> Boys of our age are kind of Casanovas. They've got their mind on other things. In my class, girls work harder.
>
> (Yvonne, a black girl)

> Girls are more mature ... I think parents bring up the girls stricter ... Boys tend to muck about, try to be big ... They can behave.
>
> (Marcia, a black girl)

Although the young black women had complaints about the immature behaviour of the boys, they also argued that some teachers held negative stereotypes about the young black men and were unable to develop appropriate strategies to deal with their non-conformist behaviour: an observation which finds resonance with the work of Driver (1979; see Chapter 3).

Boys tend to muck about ... There's a stereotype for black boys – noisy, rude, the law.

The teacher should sort of understand, you know, understand what they are really like, and then they would get on good ... 'cos, like if a coloured boy came in ... and messes about, the teacher gets angry, which I agree [with], but if they sort of just ignore the boy – the coloured boy – he'll go and sit down, and be quiet and behave himself.

(Yvette, a black girl)

Differences in the educational experience of the black girls and boys were reflected in one educational outcome: performance in public examinations. Black girls scored, on average, the equivalent of one good O level or two CSEs more than the boys. If the comparison is extended to black girls and boys in the highest ability band, the girls out-performed the boys by the equivalent of two O levels or three CSEs. The differences between the examination scores of white girls and boys were minimal.

DIMENSIONS OF CLASS

The findings from the research suggested that there were class-related differences between the educational experiences of girls in the two single-sex schools studied. Girls at Crossland experienced a curriculum closely approximating to that of a secondary modern school of the Crowther (1959) tradition: designed to meet the future domestic needs of working-class girls. Girls at the grammar school, Christchurch, experienced an academic curriculum of the uncompromising 'Miss Beale' tradition which emphasized the academic and intellectual development of young middle-class women and aimed at enabling them to become economically independent.

Findings from the research also suggested that the schools tended to assume that all Afro-Caribbean children were working class – an issue compounded by the fact that many Afro-Caribbean children, such as those in this study, attend schools in inner-city, predominately working-class areas. Undoubtedly, the perceptions that the schools had about black children influenced expectations about examination performance and career opportunities. Many of the black girls – particularly those whose families had originated from islands other than Jamaica – had very high expectations: expectations which were not matched by the school. Karen's parents, for example, had moved from middle-class occupations in Guyana to lower-status jobs in the UK and had high aspirations for their daughter.

They'd [parents] both like the idea of computing 'cos they say it's a job of the future, and we just discuss where I could go, and what college and all that stuff, so they do help me a lot ... My dad works for Ford and my mum works for the Church of England Children's Society as a secretary ... In Guyana, well my dad worked for the Ministry of Internal Affairs, I think ... I'm not really interested in having children. But she [mum] does say to wait till you've got your qualifications and get a good job and everything before you're thinking of getting married and having children.

(Karen, a black girl; family from Guyana)

Christine's family had also originated from Guyana. She complained that the careers teacher's view about what she should do had been limited by the fact that her mother now worked in a biscuit factory. She was determined, however, to challenge those expectations:

She [mum] believes that we should all get as much education as we want, and we should get qualified and be professional or whatever, because she didn't have the chance when she was at school, so she feels that we should, you know. 'Cos my sister's gone to college now, getting her A levels, and I'm going to college when I finish here, if I get my O levels, and she feels that we should get as much education as we can. She says she knows me, she says I'd be a good solicitor because I'm always arguing, you know, she thinks it will be right for me ... She works in a factory packing biscuits ... When I told that, the careers woman, right, she seems to think that you wanna do what your parents do, but you wanna better yourself don't you? If your mum's packing biscuits in a factory, you want something better than that, don't you, obviously?

(Christine, a black girl; family from Guyana)

Although schools may have had limited expectations about the girls, many, such as Sharon, experienced positive role models from outside school, within their own families and circle of friends:

My mum's always talking about staying on. She comes from Barbados, she'd like to go back there ... She just tells me to get my education and get a good job and things like that ... My dad doesn't really say much about anything ... My sister, she brings home newspapers and helps me, she phones up for things, she gives me leaflets. I've got a cousin who's very bright and she's got a good job and knows what she wants and things. I wouldn't mind being like her ... She used to be an antique dealer ... She travels a lot, she worked in Sweden. She's thinking about going to Barbados now and being a teacher. She helps us a lot as well. I admire her, she's really nice. My mum raised her.

(Sharon, a black girl; family from Barbados)

The research found differences between the examination performance of Afro-Caribbean girls. Girls from Barbados and Guyana scored an average one to two O levels, or equivalent, higher than girls where families had originated from Jamaica. Such differences may be related to the status of their parents before immigration to the UK – a finding supported by Foner (1978), Bagley (1975) and Bagley, Mallick and Verma (1979). Many Jamaican immigrants to the UK in the 1950s and 1960s were from rural areas and had received few educational opportunities compared to immigrants from Guyana and Barbados, who had often been more highly educated and had occupied middle-class occupations in the Caribbean.

As well as differences in examination performance between the young black women, there were clear differences in expectation. The young black women whose families originated from Guyana or Barbados expressed greater determination to gain qualifications, and, although they were equally critical about aspects of their school experience, were less hostile to school than the black girls of Jamaican origin.

Although there were clear differences between the expectations of the different groups of black girls (and their final examination results), which appeared related to parental background, parents from Jamaica also set a high premium on education which influenced their daughters as is illustrated in the following extract:

> The subjects we do and the opportunities we got, she didn't get that . . . She says I must try and . . . get myself good qualifications. She says you must hold up your head and get on with your work . . . [about children] she says you should wait until, uhm, all your exams, like that. Get your job. But she doesn't mind really.
>
> (Veronica, a black girl; family from Jamaica)

Safia Mirza (1992) has suggested that class factors have frequently been ignored in studies of black children in the UK. In particular, she has argued that the practice of using the Registrar-General's classifications of male heads of household as a way of determining social class has ignored the critical role of black women. In a school-based study of south London girls which she conducted in 1984, she reclassified the pupils on the basis of mother's occupation and found striking differences between the ascribed social class of black and white girls, as is shown in Table 4.2. Safia Mirza's argument was that schools ascribed inappropriate classifications to black girls and limited their expectations accordingly: an argument which accords with the findings of this research.

Table 4.2 Registrar-General's classification by mother's occupation

Classificiation (by mother's occupation)	Black girls	White girls
Professional/intermediate/managerial	44%	13%
Skilled manual/semi-skilled	48%	64%

Source: adapted from Safia Mirza (1992)

ONE EDUCATIONAL OUTCOME: EXAMINATION PERFORMANCE

As well as using material from interviews and questionnaires, the original research study also analysed the examination performance of pupils and highlighted some interesting differences between groups of pupils, some of which have already been mentioned. Comparison of examination performance between girls in the three schools presented some interesting similarities and differences which are presented in Table 4.3. The analysis suggests that at both Crossland and Greenvale there was little difference between the results of black and white girls. At Christchurch however, there was a considerable difference between the scores of black and white girls – 9 points, almost the equivalent of two additional O levels.

Table 4.3 Mean examination scores of female pupils who completed the questionnaire[2,3] (June 1981)

	Black mean	[n]	White mean	[n]	All mean	[n]
Greenvale	14.38	[8]	13.66	[18]	13.88	[26]
Crossland	13.31	[48]	14.08	[25]	13.58	[73]
Christchurch	23.13	[8]	31.95	[43]	30.57	[51]
All	14.67	[64]	22.90	[86]	19.39	[150]

Source: Riley (1985a)

The higher overall results for both black and white girls at Christchurch compared with Crossland and Greenvale was not unexpected, given Christchurch's selective intake. The results were therefore also analysed by comparing the performance of Band 1 girls at Greenvale and Crossland with those at Christchurch.[4] This analysis is presented in Table 4.4. Although it is based on a very small sample from Greenvale and Crossland, it shows a somewhat different picture, suggesting minimal differences between the performances of black girls overall, although a striking difference between the examination scores of black and white girls at Christchurch. This raises the question of why?

Table 4.4 Mean examination scores of the questionnaire sample (Band 1 girls) compared with those in the 5th year in each school (June 1981)

	The sample						Fifth year	
	Black mean	[n]	White mean	[n]	Total mean	[n]	mean	[n]
Greenvale	21.00	[1]	27.00	[1]	24.00	[2]	23.50	[21]
Crossland	20.66	[3]	20.00	[2]	20.40	[5]	14.90	[8]
Christchurch	23.13	[8]	31.95	[43]	30.57	[51]	31.10	[78]

Source: Riley (1985a)

I am not going to speculate on the reasons for such differences, or on the differences between the performance of black girls and boys mentioned earlier in the chapter. The interviews provide some clues but may not give the whole picture. The point of this presentation has been to demonstrate the importance of systematic analysis, monitoring and feedback, not only of the performance of pupils overall, or of individual pupils, but also of groups of pupils. If feedback and analysis is limited to the performance of pupils as a whole, differences and issues for exploration will be masked and the opportunity to develop strategies to tackle inequality will be lost. This critical issue about monitoring for quality and equality is explored in more detail in Chapter 6.

OUTCOMES AND INTER-RELATIONSHIPS

Issues of race, class and gender impacted on the school experience of the girls in the research study. The inter-relationship of these factors was complex and pupils' assessment of their school experience depended on a complex set of factors. At Greenvale issues of gender and race affected their school experience. The gender barriers were the immediate and tangible institutional obstacles which they had to overcome in their daily lives. The institutional obstacles created by racism at Greenvale were more hidden, and it may well be that, as the black girls themselves reported, teacher and pupil racism was much more directed towards the black boys.

At Crossland and Christchurch issues of gender equality were taken for granted, although the lack of specific strategies to counteract the traditional bias in the curriculum offered to the girls was particularly restrictive for the Crossland girls. At Christchurch the invisibility of the black girls created tensions for them and ensured that the often narrow perceptions of the white girls remained unchallenged.

One of the most striking differences between the black and white girls in the study was in their overall views about school. The majority of the black girls interviewed (27 out of 42) described their school experience overall as predominantly negative – a view shared by only a majority of white girls (9 out of 24). Safia Mirza (1992) summed up the experience of black girls in terms that could equally apply to my own research:

> Black girls were not only impeded by teachers' assessments of their abilities, but their decision-making was fundamentally influenced by the poverty of advice and information that they received about job opportunities.
>
> (Safia Mirza, 1992, p. 192)

A further aspect that needs appreciation, in my experience, is the resourcefulness of the young women – often unappreciated by their schools – and their determination to gain qualifications and succeed in the labour market.

The school experience of the young black women in this study cannot be summarized as simply the addition of racism to the effects of class and gender on white girls' experiences. The inter-relationship is more complex. In particular, the gender aspect is different for black girls because of the differences between black culture and the traditional white patriarchy.[5] The research findings suggest that a number of young black women were able to challenge male domination and also reject motions of female economic and social dependence on men.

In all three schools young black women showed greater resistance than young white women to gender stereotyping. That resistance manifested itself in a number of ways, perhaps most clearly in the perceptions that the young black women had about their own economic independence and in their belief in qualifications as a 'bankable commodity' – a 'good' to be acquired and saved for future long-term use.

Central to the school experience of the black girls in this study was racism, occasionally overt but more usually hidden. This created conflict and tension for some black girls – particularly those at Christchurch – between their experience of a school ethos that effectively turned a colour-blind eye to racism and their own positive assertions of themselves as young, female and black in a society they knew to be racist. For them the struggle was to become visible.

The main conclusion from the research remains that issues of race, gender and class are profoundly complicating factors in the British educational system. None can be considered merely as an additional aspect of school life that can be considered or dealt with apart from the other aspects. Yet consideration of all three together raises contradictions and ambivalence.

Young white women in inner-city areas often have to grapple with limited school and home expectations. In different ways, Greenvale and Crossland offered limited school opportunities: girls were invisible at Greenvale and experienced a limited domesticated curriculum at Crossland. Both experiences reinforced many societal views about women. Whilst the aspirations of white girls may have been raised at Christchurch, black girls lost out.

The young black women in this study were not just amalgams of stereotypes. They were individuals with a range of aptitudes and aspirations that had arisen from, or in some cases survived an educational system that did not understand them.

TEN YEARS ON

What resonance do we find with this agenda a decade or so later? Early in 1993 I visited a coeducational south London school, Marchbank, to explore some of these issues with a group of ten black and white girls in Year 11 (5th-year students, as they were then known). I chose Marchbank for two reasons. First, Marchbank had been established some years previously as a coeducational school – an amalgamation of two schools, one boys' and one girls'. The girls' school had been Crossland. Second, my knowledge of south London school catchment areas led me to believe that Marchbank drew its pupils from local areas and communities similar to those of the three schools in my original study.

I have drawn on the interview material from Marchbank not to make direct comparisons with my original research but to highlight themes and issues of contemporary relevance. I talked to the girls about their experience of Marchbank and their expectations for the future. They were lively and challenging, keen to know what their counterparts had said some ten years previously and candid about their assessment of the school and their evaluation about their own prospects for the future.

Girls at Marchbank

Visible or invisible? The girls argued that there was no longer discrimination in the overt curriculum: 'There's no such thing as boys' subjects and girls' subjects.' All students had taken design, technical drawing and woodwork and there were more boys than girls doing home economics. Performing arts was the only subject taken predominantly by girls: 'The boys are not into acting, singing and dancing.'

Their complaints were about the hidden curriculum: the ways the boys dominated school, and the organizational arrangements that sustained their domination. In their view the boys were consistently rowdy and demanded and received greater attention from the teachers. As the boys grew up, however, this became less of a problem:

> In the lower years the boys can be childish but now they're growing up.
>
> I feel that they get more attention from the teachers ... They're rowdy whilst the girls are more mature.
>
> They can gain more attention because on the whole they're louder ... they don't shut up until they get attention and the teachers just have to deal with them.
>
> They get more attention because they're slower to learn – not all the boys but the majority of them.
>
> Sometimes in this school you wish you were in an all-girls' school and that there weren't any boys in the school, but another time you think it's all right.

This constant classroom domination by the boys caused great frustration and sometimes resulted in the girls resorting to similar tactics in order to get attention:

> You can only get attention in the class if you mess about.
>
> When I talk to her [the teacher] nicely and I'm doing my work, she marks the boys'. So sometimes I just mess about. You get really frustrated.
>
> You get fed up of waiting.
>
> Just because you're bright doesn't mean that you shouldn't get attention. The bright ones are always left to the last.

There were occasions, however, when this was not a problem:

> When the boys can handle the work, they're not so disruptive.
>
> In science they do the work better because they enjoy it more.
>
> They're better in smaller groups because when they're in bigger groups they're trying to prove themselves, 'Oh, I can shout the loudest.' There's only four in my group now. It's better when they're separated from their mates.
>
> It depends on the group. In our science group there are only thirteen

students – four of these are boys – and so the boys are outnumbered, they have to behave.

The girls shared a view that they were more able and harder-working than boys:

> In science girls are better than the boys.
>
> In science you go in groups and if there's say two girls and two boys, the girls do all the work ... They don't do no work and just go along with what you say and write it down.
>
> You hear so much prejudice about boys being better at maths and science. In this school it's the opposite. Mr X says you should make the science class all girls because they're much better ... We get the grades.

The girls also complained about the boys' offensive behaviour to them, although they also argued that the different forms of harassment which they had been subjected to over the years had come from only a small minority of boys.

> It was bad in the third year but it still goes on. You still get the odd one or two.
>
> But there's another thing: this boy, X, you know when he comes up to hug you up, right, and you don't want to be hugged up, or something, he says, 'what's wrong with me?', and it's like you're obligated to them or something. That's what I don't like ... Gets on my nerves and you don't want to start an argument.
>
> After a while they get on your nerves. You tell them once but they get rude after a while. They think that you like it when you say go away. You're just trying to be nice to them, by saying 'go away', but then you just have to start being rude.
>
> The most common thing is they call you is flat-chested, or that sort of thing, or the other way round is big-chested.
>
> Or if they don't get what they want, they start cursing you and calling you offensive names: boggle-eyed and picky head, ugly and mean. They say there are no nice and good-looking girls in this school.

But the girls reserved their greatest indignation for the way that they had been treated by some boys and some members of staff in their endeavours to establish a girls' football team.

> There's a girls' football team *now* but there wasn't one before.
>
> There was a prime example this morning [of the school's attitude]. The other years [the boys' teams] have all got matches next week but we've got a match this evening. They told them that the boys had got a match but they didn't tell anyone that we've got a match.
>
> Another thing about the boys is you tell them that you're going to play

football or certain things, they laugh at you, they just assume it's a boys' game.

There's some boys that take you seriously but the majority of boys think you're stupid, that you can't play.

I've never even thought of playing football [at break-times] because there's nowhere to play.

We never play at lunchtime because all the boys have got all the football pitches and to play you literally have to beg them, or if they do let you play, you might as well not be there because they pass it between the boys.

They even take over the netball pitches.

We play after school and we tell them [the boys] that day is our particular day for coming in but they still take over.

When we suggested a girls' football team, Miss A said she wouldn't go along with it because she believes it's a boys' game.

But Mr B he opens the changing rooms for us, gives us the footballs and the football kits, and the woman teacher says it's a boys' game.

The boys get a trainer. We don't, we train ourselves. Some man comes down from Millwall. They get everything, they get new strip but we only got a strip because it was free. But we still have only got half the strip because the boys took it and nothing was said about it. And still today we still haven't got the kit.

Two issues emerged from this profoundly negative experience for the girls. The first was the resilience of the girls themselves. They had challenged attitudes and resistance from staff and pupils and had formed a girls' team, which played against girls from other schools. The second was the importance to the girls of the staff who supported them (the male PE teacher and the headteacher) and who, in their view, challenged sexist stereotypes.

For all of the girls interviewed, the headteacher, Miss C, was a significant figure in their school lives, one whose model of leadership they respected and one who projected a strong view about the role of women in society.[6] It was through approaching the headteacher that the girls had finally got permission to set up the football team. 'We told the headteacher that it wasn't fair and that we wanted to play and she agreed and said it should happen.' In their view, Miss C had improved the school considerably and created a very different atmosphere from the previous headteachers:

The headteacher that was here, Mr X, he was rubbish and Miss Y, a woman teacher, would go up to Mr X. He wouldn't listen to her. It was really weird, but he listened to the men. A couple of teachers told us that and we didn't believe it but we saw it for ourselves after a while. The problems that were noted by women teachers, nothing was done about it. He was sexist.

The school used to be rubbish but I think it's improving.

It's improved since Miss C came. She's made a lot of changes. Some of them we didn't like – she got rid of the pips between lessons. But she realized that it wasn't working and she brought them back. If we say to her we're not happy about these things, she'll normally go and sort it out. She'll compromise. She's made lots of changes about uniform, it's more stricter now.

She's made the school more presentable. Put in decent windows about the school.

This school has got a lot of computers. It's only over the last few months. It's Miss C again, she got them.

I don't want to swell her head too much but she has done a lot of good for this school, more than anyone else.

Race and racism Both black and white girls were very positive in their assertions about the multiracial nature of the school population. They also spoke of the school's anti-racist and anti-sexist policies but argued that such racism as existed within the school was challenged by the pupils themselves, rather than staff:

I think this school's quite good because they've got a lot of different nationalities like around this table.

I don't really know anyone whose parents have brought them up to hate other people because of their race.

I don't think, like deep down in their heart people have got a deep hatred because of colour.

Some people might be racist but this school doesn't promote it.

You may not be racist but you may in an argument come out with something racist which you don't mean.

[In this school] if they're racist they wouldn't get away with it. Maybe they would if they were sexist.

But it's not sorted out by the teachers, it's sorted out in the classroom, because if someone's racist, everyone's going to hate them.

If someone cussed a black person, the whole of the school used to get on to them.

But that doesn't happen to other races. It only happens to black people because there're more black people in the school . . . If someone cusses a Chinese person not everyone would go up and complain.

You know they've got that rule now that if you're racist or sexist you get expelled.

What would this school be like if we were all the same? It would be really boring. It's nice to have all the differences.

They suggested, however, like the girls at Greenvale, that things were somewhat different for the black boys:

Miss D, she picks on black boys when they're new. They come in, they just act big and she just assumes that when a new black person comes in it's trouble. It's the way they walk, or dress, they've got their string vest hanging down to the bottom of their knees. So it's like she's warning them off, don't even think about it.

The problem is that some teachers in this school use their power too much.

Future aspirations All of the girls planned to continue their education, either at college or at school. Their career aspirations were fairly wide-ranging, but like those of their peers of a decade ago, largely fell into occupations that could be classified as traditionally female: health visitor, social worker, nursery nurse, nursery teacher, something in computers, designer, chef, fashion and beauty consultant, scientist, doctor, advertising executive. But in talking about their career aspirations all of the young women asserted a strong determination to achieve their goals and also to achieve economic and social independence – an objective strongly supported by their mothers. Families, marriage, partnerships were not immediate issues:

That's the last thing on my mind. I want to get an education and a decent job and a home and you can think about that afterwards.

For me, my career comes first. My mum says I should get as much education as I can because it's difficult to come back.

A lot of you say you don't want to have kids and that your education comes first but you don't know.

My mum never achieved what she wanted to do but she wants me to achieve.

My mum [says] when she was younger there were no options open to her, it was either get married or nothing. So she married my dad and my dad let her have a career but at any time he could have said, 'Right, that's it, you're not working anymore.' She says if I want to get married at any time she'll support me but she'd rather I didn't because it's a trap which you don't need.

You've got more obligations if you've got a family. You've got to think about your husband when he comes in, you've got to think about your children. They've got to have some dinner, they want some clothes, they want to go on holiday. It's hard.

If we're all equal that's OK. But someone shouldn't be put down if they don't want to have a career. What's wrong with a bloke or a woman who wants to look after their kids?

But what's wrong if you want a career?

The point is that everything should be your choice.

Labour market The girls spoke of the difficulties which friends and members of their family found in gaining employment. Their determination to gain qualifications and achieve economic independence was influenced by their understanding about limited opportunities in the labour market:

> Everyone wants to go into further education but there's no jobs out there.
>
> But you need qualifications to have a try. It's really important.

The girls also argued that sexism and racism were barriers to their employment opportunities. Central government had failed to challenge racism and sexism and, in the view of several girls, had contributed to the climate of racism in the labour market. They did not argue for special pleading but for opportunities which reflected their capabilities.

Sexism

> I did this assignment about prejudice, values, attitudes and beliefs and that all comes under the same issue – prejudice. There was one question – 'would you employ a woman plumber?' I interviewed twelve people, six older women and men and six younger women and men, and all the men said no, they might employ her as a last resort: women can't handle being a plumber. The women said it doesn't matter as long as they can do the job.
>
> Some people believe that women should be employed just because they're a woman but that's not right either.
>
> Some employers take on women just to show they're all right ... A few lovely ladies in the office or something really stupid.
>
> The system stereotypes people. Some people think a secretary is automatically a woman.
>
> But a male nurse, or hairdresser, they think they're gay.

Racism

> I think in the government in this day and age, it all boils down to colour.
>
> Yes, [racism] is always an issue, although all employers aren't like that. It's the minority spoil it for the majority.
>
> You only see the bad things in the press, say like someone is sacked because he's Asian. But they don't show you all the races working together, you don't see that, you just get the bad publicity.

The home The girls held strong views about equality in the labour market and equality at home. In their view, to achieve equality in the future both girls and boys had to learn to share domestic chores. Education should prepare both girls and boys for their future shared domestic roles and parents needed to ensure that boys took their equal share in domestic chores: something they anticipated that they would insist on if they became parents.

But domestic things are important – education isn't going to wash your clothes.

Boys think shoving a pizza in the oven is dinner.

Some parents think it's just girls who should learn these things.

My brother doesn't do a thing. I have to do everything. My mum doesn't tell him.

My brother he's disgusting. Everyone's got chores. But I always end up doing things. I said to my mum, 'I'll have a dishwasher for my birthday, I might as well, as I do all the washing up.'

If I have kids I'm going to have equal opportunities.

If they don't wash up they won't get any dinner.

It should be the same for the boys and girls.

I asked the young women, if I returned and interviewed girls at their school or a similar school in ten years' time, how they would have liked things to change.

No racism, no sexism, equal rights.

The things that we want, they're impossible unless you've got a perfect world.

But people might think we're greedy just wanting equal rights. But it shouldn't be greedy but it should be how the world should be.

We want too much but the boys just get it automatically.

But it's not too much being equal.

Marchbank: Issues for the future

Three issues emerged from the experience, attitudes and expectations of the young women at Marchbank. The first was the degree to which the boys in the school still dominated classroom time and space: teachers responded to the rowdiness of the boys by giving them greater attention. Bright and hard-working girls were ignored and occasionally themselves resorted to strategies of disruption in order to gain the attention of the teacher. Boys also dominated playground space and sporting activities such as football, and subjected girls, at certain times of their school life, to different degrees of harassment.

All of this echoed many of the experiences of young women at Greenvale ten years earlier. But in two areas there had been significant changes. The first was in the assertive and self-reliant attitudes of the girls themselves – black and white. As Riddell (1992) found (see p. 44), the language of feminism had entered the classroom. The girls challenged the sexist attitudes of a previous male headteacher and a current female teacher. They wanted 'no racism, no sexism, equal rights': opportunities to have a career, or to choose not to have a career. They valued their autonomy and independence and were determined to pursue educational opportunities, in spite of their awareness of the lack of job opportunities and of racism and sexism in the labour market.

Another evident change lay in the impact of the school itself. Marchbank was a school in which the pupils knew that racism would not be tolerated and although they argued that challenges to racism came from the pupils themselves rather than the staff, they were equally clear that the school had a clear policy on racism and sexism. It was also very clear that the young women both acknowledged and valued the strong leadership role played by the female headteacher. Here was someone who in their view had begun to turn the school around in a style that treated them positively (she had sorted out the football) and sensitively (she was prepared to compromise and listen to them). She represented a strong and powerful model for change.

NOTES

1. Because of the diversity of backgrounds and experiences of pupils in Category C, an analysis of their experience is excluded from this chapter. A complex range of factors influenced their school experience, which schools would need to unpack in the same way as for other groups of children.

2. The analysis of examination results allocated each pupil a total examination score based on a scale used at that time by the ILEA, which allocated 5 points to a CSE 1 or O level grade C (see Table 4.5).

Table 4.5 ILEA Research and Statistics Performance Scale for O level and CSE examinations

O level grade	Score	CSE grade
A	7	
B	6	
C	5	1
D	4	2
E	3	3
	2	4
	1	5

3. The examination results collected were for 5th-year performance only and thus did not span the potential examination period for O levels and CSE., i.e. 4th and 6th years. Additionally, the average examination results for the pupils who completed the questionnaire included those pupils who had not been entered for examinations, or had received no score. Exclusion of those groups would obviously have resulted in a higher average score.

4. The ILEA 'banding' system was used to help allocate children to secondary schools. Pupils were assigned to Bands 1, 2 or 3 on the basis of primary school judgements, and performance on general intelligence tests on verbal reasoning: Band 1 was the highest rating. The purpose of this was to achieve a balanced intake in comprehensive schools. The system attracted some criticism. Bagley (1975), for example, criticized banding because of its dependence on teachers' assessment of

pupils and suggested that teachers misjudged the abilities of black pupils (black children were under-represented in Bands 1 and 2).

5. The term 'patriarchy' has been little used in this book because of its limited capacity to explain the position of black women. Carby (1982), for example, has argued that patriarchy is based on a model of female economic and social dependency on men that is inappropriate to black women.

6. At no time did I ask the girls any questions about the headteacher. All of the girls' comments about Miss C emerged unprompted through discussions on other issues.

PART III

PRESCRIPTION FOR ACTION

Chapter 5

Leadership

EDUCATIONAL LEADERSHIP: THE CONTEXT

There are two certainties about the management of the education service of the future. The first is that organizations – schools, colleges, local authorities, funding agencies – will continue to change. The second is that the leaders of those organizations – headteachers, principals, directors – will have to manage the change process and establish new expectations.

The educational leaders of the future will be a diverse group, not only in terms of their background and experience but also in terms of their responsibilities and powers. The challenges they face will be complex and taxing. The actions they take to shape, to influence and to inform their organizations will affect the *process* of schooling – the nature of the education experience offered to young people – and the *outcomes* – how they feel about themselves as young people and how equipped they are to move forward into adulthood.

The management tasks of organizational leaders in local education authorities will be less focused on direct outcomes than in the past. They will need to redirect their activities from the management of action to the management of influence. Headteachers and principals will have the opportunity to exercise their leadership through more direct activities and intervention but they will also be subject to a range of external constraints and influences.

Who will assume these leadership roles and what kinds of values will underpin their management activities? Legislation has introduced market values into the system, but the individualistic values of the marketplace conflict with other more collectivist, or community-based goals. Concerns about meeting the needs of children may clash with activities aimed at responding to the demands of individual clients. Concepts such as partnership and collegiality conflict with notions of individual rights. It is the new leaders in the education system who will have to balance these competing goals.

The purpose of this chapter is to explore issues of leadership within the education service:

- What are the pathways to leadership and what are the characteristics of the leaders themselves?
- What are the implications for staff, or for pupils, of different forms of leadership?
- Do women and men lead in the same way?
- What are the implications of these issues for the future leadership of the education service?

EDUCATIONAL LEADERS: NATIONAL AND INTERNATIONAL COMPARISONS

Although there are variations in the pattern of representation of women in positions of educational leadership, both within the European Community and internationally, three common trends emerge:

- Our educational leaders are predominantly white and male.
- At all levels, in virtually all countries, women are under-represented at managerial level.
- The proportion of women employed in teaching declines as the age of the students rises.

In most countries, school-teaching is a predominantly female occupation. Teaching is by no means, however, as predominantly a female profession internationally as it is in Europe or North America. According to Davies (1990), the gender balance in developing and Commonwealth countries ranges from below 10 per cent female, in countries such as Bangladesh and Nepal, to over 80 per cent in the Philippines and parts of the Caribbean.

Within Europe the percentage of female primary school teachers ranges from 80 per cent in the UK to just under 50 per cent in Germany. Except in Portugal, where 90 per cent of the primary school heads or principals are women, women are poorly represented in the top leadership roles. In the UK women occupy just over 40 per cent of primary headships. The most dramatic disparities are in Denmark and the Netherlands:

- In Denmark women constitute 57 per cent of primary school teachers but only 1 per cent of principals are women.
- In the Netherlands, 65 per cent of the primary teaching force is female but only 12 per cent of principals are women.

(OECD, 1985/6)

At secondary school level, women constitute about half the teaching force (except in the Netherlands, where they form 27 per cent) but again are substantially under-represented as principals or headteachers. The percentage of women secondary headteachers, or principles, ranges from 4 per cent in the Netherlands to 43.5 per cent in Greece (OECD, 1985/6). Within the UK there is a big difference between Scotland, where 3.5 per cent of the headteachers are women, and England and Wales, where 15.7 per cent are women (Gerver and Hart, 1990).

Unpublished figures from the Department for Education leaked to a national paper suggested that ethnic minority groups are seriously under-represented in teaching. Only 3.3 per cent of full-time teachers are from black and ethnic minority groups, although 5.5 per cent of the population are from ethnic minority groups (*Times Educational Supplement*, 12.3.1992).[1] The position for black women teachers is acute. A survey carried out by the Commission for Racial Equality, for example, revealed that only 3 per cent of ethnic minority women were in headteacher or deputy headteacher posts but that 80 per cent of black women teachers were on the basic teaching grade (main professional grade) without any allowances, compared with 62 per cent of white women (Ranger, 1988).

Higher education remains almost entirely a male preserve. A survey of 11 institutions in the old university sector carried out in 1993 found that although women made up nearly half the student population and over one-fifth of the total academic workforce, only 4.9 per cent of professors were women. The survey also found that women professors were paid on average £1,500 a year less than their male colleagues (Association of University Teachers, 1993, p. 1).

The lack of representation of women in formal positions of leadership in the education service is problematic from a number of vantage points. It suggests that the talents and skills of many women in the education service are not being adequately recognized, and it serves to reinforce stereotypes in our society. If young women and men are not accustomed to seeing women in positions of authority and men in positions of support, this will limit their view about the capabilities of women and men. The inadequate representation of women in educational leadership will affect many other areas of employment.

PATHWAYS TO LEADERSHIP

The education service has long provided a vehicle for employment and independence for single women. It has also provided an opportunity for some of those women leaders to exercise different forms of leadership and pursue varying goals. The late nineteenth century provided an opportunity for such leadership models to emerge. Most distinctive of these were the leadership models of the Misses Beale and Buss. Dorothy Beale founded Cheltenham Ladies' College in a tradition which sought to enhance 'the Victorian feminine ideal'. Cheltenham, a school 'rooted in the values of the conservative leisure class' and the Anglican Church, aimed to provide an education for the daughters of the upper classes which stressed feminine accomplishments and a degree of academic expertise.

Miss Buss, who founded both North London Collegiate and Camden Girls' School, established a very different education tradition, one aimed at enabling young women to become economically independent. Both North London Collegiate and Camden Girls' emphasized the academic and intellectual development of young women and provided a pattern for many girls' day schools and girls' grammar schools founded after the 1902 Education Act (Lavigueur, 1980).

Given the strong traditions of educational leadership provided by these and other nineteenth-century women educationalists, why in the twentieth century are women still not appointed to leadership positions to the same degree as men? Davies (1990) has suggested that one of the reasons for this is that, internationally, education management is conceptualized in a way that excludes women.[2] From her research on education management in developing and Commonwealth countries, she concluded that:

● men perform more managerial tasks in school than women;
● men take ownership of public decision-making by assuming responsibility for the 'hard' managerial tasks;

- men are more confident about their capacity to perform managerial tasks whether or not they can actually perform them; and
- some men adopt a noticeable language style which stresses competition, material reward and status.

Whilst men are taking on the apparently 'harder' managerial tasks, women are in the more private or personal areas of school life, such as pupil welfare and home–school liaison. Once they become organizational leaders, women put great emphasis on the needs and expectations of the people in their organization. Men are more concerned with administrative tasks, budgets and relationships with their superiors (Lundgren, 1986).

The road to leadership is very different for women and men. Men are encouraged at an earlier stage than women to apply for senior educational posts and are given more opportunities to experience leadership roles (Leithwood, Steinbach and Begley, 1991). Women's skills and experiences are not sufficiently recognized in the jobs they do, or as fitting them for the jobs for which they might aspire.

There is also evidence to suggest that women and men report their management responsibilities differently. Women express less confidence in their ability to assume a leadership role and have less confidence in their knowledge, skills and personal qualities (Ouston, Gold and Gosling, 1992).

> Men think they would be good at jobs even if they don't do them: women express less certainty about their competence, even in areas where they have shown themselves to be competent.
>
> (Davies, 1990, p. 8)

Shakeshaft (1990), in her work on educational administration in the USA, constructs this issue differently. She suggests that, because of their socialization, women are more likely than men to have the skills needed for educational administration; men have to learn them. Women focus on the skills, talents and needs of people within an organization and understand how to pull these together in some common purpose. Men may know about budgets but they have to learn about people.

Within the UK there is growing evidence to suggest that the characteristics which are associated with successful management of the education service are becoming more, rather than less, associated with male rather than female traits. The increasing emphasis on technical and financial managerial skills and on budgetary controls is reinforcing the tendency for men to be viewed as more suitable candidates for management. The consequence of this is that despite the increase in women in middle management over the last decade, there has been a decrease in the percentage of women appointed as headteachers or deputies (Migniuolo and De Lyon, 1989).

There is substantial evidence to suggest that despite the Equal Pay Act introduced in 1975, women still experience discrimination in their pay. An EOC report on differentials in pay between women and men highlighted the point that the gap between women's and men's pay is wider in the UK than in any other European country. On average, women in the UK earn 77 per cent of their male counterparts' salaries. The pay disparities continue even when women reach management positions. The report also found that whilst 52 per cent of male office managers earned £350 per week or more, only 16 per cent of female managers earned that amount (Equal Opportunities Commission, 1991).

New pay structures and new expectations about suitable middle managers of our schools (heads of department, heads of year) are also restricting the opportunities available to women. A survey carried out by the National Union of Teachers found that women teachers were less likely than men teachers to have benefited from the additional responsibility allowances created by the Teachers' Pay and Conditions Act 1987. The survey also found that the allowances were usually allocated without competitive interview but where, in the minority of cases, such an interview took place, women did slightly better than men.

> Although 48 per cent of secondary school teachers are female, only 8.4 per cent receive the highest responsibility allowance D/E, compared with 30.9 per cent of their male colleagues.
>
> (NUT, 1990)

Al-Khalifa and Widdowson Migniuolo (1990) have also suggested that women teachers take on the same or similar duties as male teachers but with less pay, despite the Equal Pay legislation.

In 1983, in response to an EC Directive, a Conservative government reluctantly made an amendment to the Equal Pay Act. The amendment introduced the concept of equal pay for work of equal value and has provided some scope for women to tackle such discrimination. In industrial tribunal cases such as *Gill* v *Doncaster* (1989) and *Hanlon* v *Kirklees* (1991) women teachers have had their discrimination acknowledged. In the *Hanlon* v *Kirklees* case, Veronica Hanlon, a teacher of English and school librarian, received nearly £5,000 in back pay when an industrial tribunal concluded that she had been paid less than a male colleague for doing work of equal value. (The male colleague had previously been offered a higher grade to run the school library.)

Despite these successful cases, the contribution that women make to the education service is frequently undervalued. Indeed, a new image of educational leadership is emerging in the UK. Leaders are tough, abrasive financial entrepreneurs managing the new competitive education markets. *Managing education organizations is increasingly seen as men's business.*[3]

This picture may not be unique to the UK. As was suggested in Chapter 2, delegation to school councils for responsibility for the appointment of headships in the state of Victoria in Australia resulted in a reduction in the number of women principals appointed to schools. Austria has experienced a similar reduction in opportunities for women. Higher-level vocational schools for domestic science and commerce, which have opened their doors to male pupils over the last few years, now offer fewer promotional opportunities for women. Although these schools still have a pupil intake which is 99 per cent female, 50 per cent of the principals are now male, compared with 30 per cent ten years ago (Ranfil-Guggenberger, 1990).

But women have an enormous contribution to make as education leaders. The rest of the chapter will examine how women lead and explore the contribution that they can make to leadership at a time of great uncertainty in education.

WOMEN AND MEN: LEADERSHIP ASPIRATIONS

> The professional literature is replete with theoretical examples explaining 'women's lesser work commitment'. Women are assumed to be less assertive, less ambitious and less career-orientated than men.
>
> (Kaufman and Fetters, 1980, p. 251)

Are women less ambitious and career-orientated than men? According to Davies's study (1990), of leadership in developing and Commonwealth countries, women and men were equally ambitious. Such a conclusion has resonance with the UK experience. Findings from a major study of 805 women and 1,497 male managers and professionals in a range of occupations (both public and private sector) in Britain similarly challenged the assumption that women have less career ambition and commitment than men (Alban Metcalfe and Nicholson, 1984).

The study found that women generally had higher qualifications than men and that women in both the public and private sector were much more concerned than men with the challenges of the job. In general, women were more concerned with factors *intrinsic* to the job, such as whether it made a contribution to society, or whether it developed them. Women were also more concerned than men to have their accomplishments appreciated, to work in a friendly environment and to have a job that fitted in with their outside life. Men tended to focus on factors which were *extrinsic* to the job, such as high earnings, fringe benefits and job security. The study concluded that differences in attitudes to jobs were more a product of gender than a product of employment in the public or private sector.

The study also illuminated the complexities for women in managing a career and a home life. Women had to make life choices which were less likely to be shared by their male colleagues. Men, for example, were more likely to be married than women: 93 per cent of males in the public sector and 93 per cent of those in the private sector, compared with 63 per cent of women in the public sector and 54 per cent in the private sector. Women were also less likely to have children. Fourteen per cent of married men in the public sector and 13 per cent in the private sector had no children, compared with 66 per cent of women in the public sector and 58 per cent in the private sector (see Table 5.1). The minority of married women who had children also tended to have fewer children than their male counterparts.

Females with partners were also more likely to be in dual career relationships than males. Eighty-five per cent of females in the public sector and 91 per cent of females in the private sector had partners in full-time employment, compared with 23 per cent and 28 per cent respectively of men in the private and public sectors.

Table 5.1 Women and men in management: life choice differences

| | Women | | Men | |
	Married	no children	Married	no children
Public sector	63 per cent	66 per cent	93 per cent	14 per cent
Private sector	54 per cent	58 per cent	93 per cent	13 per cent

Source: Alban Metcalfe and Nicholson (1984)

The pattern for women in education management appears to be little different from the overall picture presented in the Alban Metcalfe and Nicholson study for managerial and professional staff across a range of occupations. According to a small Scottish study of 24 women in educational management (in schools, higher education institutions and local authorities), senior women in education gained their appointments later than their male counterparts, regardless of whether they had taken career breaks. Although most of the women in the study had been or were married, fewer than half had children. Women also tended to have what have been described as 'tapestried' careers, moving from one profession or area of work to related areas, rather than progressing through traditional hierarchies. They viewed their career moves as fortuitous, rather than planned, although they claimed to have built on all the opportunities which luck presented to them (Gerver and Hart, 1990). Research findings on the characteristics of women leaders and on their pathways to leadership are summarized in Figure 5.1.

The notion of tapestried careers is an interesting one. It presents a rich image of women's working lives: building up expertise in an area and translating that expertise into other areas of work. It implies flexibility and the ability to transfer skills and knowledge. Given the continuing changes in the context and organization of education, such broad career patterns have much to offer for the leadership of the education service.

The research evidence puts paid to the myth that women are less ambitious than men. Although the senior women in education management no longer have to give up teaching if they marry, if they are to develop their careers they still have to make life-choice decisions which their male colleagues do not have to make.

STYLES OF LEADERSHIP

The figure of the 'Miss Buss' or 'Miss Beale' dedicated to the education and welfare of young women may not have entirely departed from the education scene, but is the style of leadership adopted by the twentieth-century Miss Buss or Beale any different from that of her male counterpart?

We have so far identified that the path to leadership differs for women and that women in senior managerial positions tend to value different aspects of their jobs as compared with men. Next we need to examine whether women and men lead in

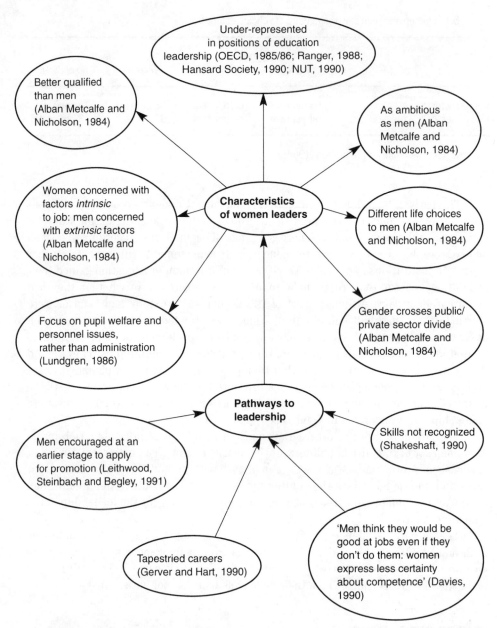

Figure 5.1 *Characteristics of women leaders, and their pathways to leadership: a summary of research findings*

different ways and the implications of any differences for the education service. Management and leadership are often thought to be synonymous. Although the two are inter-related, there is a clear distinction: leadership involves a perspective on how to influence the behaviour of individuals or groups within an organization and how to achieve outcomes; management is the process by which leadership is accomplished.

Management theorists have explored various concepts of leadership over the last decade or so. The concepts of transactional and transformational leadership have been particularly useful to this exploration.

- *Transactional* leaders view job performance as a series of transactions with subordinates through which rewards are exchanged for services provided, or punishments given for inadequate rewards. The power of the transactional leader is drawn from the organization itself and the formal authority which the leader has through holding their particular post in the organization.
- *Transformational leaders* work to get staff to transform their own self-interest into broader organizational interests and goals. As leaders they are democratic, people-orientated and have a participative decision-making style. The leaders themselves attribute their power to hard work, or interpersonal skills, rather than to their formal position in the organization.

(McGregor Burns, 1978)

An American study of female and male leaders (Rosener, 1990) suggested that women are more likely to be transformational than transactional leaders, although they are able to switch from being transformational to transactional leaders if participation does not work. Rosener argued that these differences spring from women's socialization and their past work experience. Historically, women have lacked formal authority over others and over resources and have therefore had to develop other ways to accomplish their objectives. Rosener also argued that women had been able to derive satisfaction from helping others, including their spouses, whilst men have had to take on other attributes.

> While men have had to appear to be competitive, strong, tough, decisive and in control, women have been allowed to be cooperative, emotional, supportive and vulnerable. This may explain why women today are more likely then men to be interactive leaders.
>
> (Rosener, 1990, p. 124)

Rosener also found that women and men described their leadership styles differently. Women were more likely than men to say that what they attempted to do was to make their staff feel important, included and energized. They did not covet formal authority, as they had learnt to live without it. Once in power, they still saw the sharing of power and information as an asset.

Rosener went on to develop her own model, *interactive leadership*, in which leaders worked to make interaction with subordinates worthwhile, to encourage participation and enhance self-worth. She described the characteristics of an interactive leader as one who:

- encourages participation;
- shares power and information;

- sees information as a two-way process;
- enhances the self-worth of others;
- has an aversion to behaviour that sets her or him apart from others; and
- energizes others through her or his own enthusiasm for their job.

Such a leadership model is not unproblematic. It takes time. It requires giving up control and can be interpreted as not having the answers. It also opens the door to criticism and conflict; and of course not everyone wants to be energized. Rosener has suggested, however, that interactive leadership may emerge as a management style for many organizations. It is a style that meets the demands of the workforce for increased participation and the demands of the economy for organizations which can adapt rapidly to change.

Given that interactive leadership may not always work, women's capacity to switch to the more directive transactional leadership becomes important. Effective leadership requires a repertoire of management styles which will allow the leader to adapt to changing circumstances and the needs of the organization. For leadership to be effective it must also be situational.[4] *Situational leadership* depends on the capacity of the leader to adapt not only to changing circumstances but to the organizational context. It is also a notion of leadership which depends on the capacity of the individual to draw on a repertoire of management styles.

Gerver and Hart (1990), in their modest Scottish research project, suggested that the predominant management style adopted by the senior women managers in their study tended to be gender neutral or androgynous. Women combined both masculine and feminine characteristics in their leadership styles.

> The extent to which our interviewees mention both feminine and masculine characteristics in their descriptions of their management style is striking. Interviewees saw themselves as flexible and firm, consultative and confrontational, caring and ruthless, competitive and democratic.
>
> (Gerver and Hart, 1990, p. 6)

These findings accord with those from a workshop which was part of a research project on how women lead in local government (Riley and White; see note 5). The seven women who contributed to the workshop were all chief executives of local authorities. In acting as leaders in their various organizations they drew on a repertoire of styles and described their behaviour as: *considerate, empathetic* and *energizing of others*, but also *intolerant, demanding, pushy* and *provocative*. In decision-making they were: *strategic and decisive*, but also *dogged and humble*. The research will go on to examine how their leadership is manifested in the workplace.

Some American studies have sought to analyse the components of the effective leadership models adopted by a number of women and examine the lessons for business. Helgesen (1990) focused on women's values, which she described as feminine principles, and which had long been dismissed as weaknesses in management. She suggested that caring, being involved, taking responsibility are all parts of women's ways of leadership and that women do not hesitate to make intuitive decisions which could be helpful to business.

WOMEN'S EXPERIENCE OF MANAGEMENT

Once women have reached senior management positions in their organizations, their troubles are far from over. As was suggested earlier (p. 89), there could well be pay differentials, but women also face many other barriers. A survey of 1,000 women managers (including managers from education departments) identified the sequence of difficulties which many women managers had to negotiate. These difficulties included:

- *Requirements.* Women may be *disbarred* by inflexible job require-ments, such as long or irregular working hours, or specific experience requirements that career breaks may have made more difficult to gain.
- *Facilities.* Women may be *deterred* by the absence of facilities such as a career break, flexitime, child-care.
- *Environment.* Women may be *demotivated* by their unsupportive workplace environment, the continued prevalence of sexual harass-ment (38.5 per cent of women in the survey had experienced sexual harassment personally, or amongst colleagues), exclusion from important networks.
- *Style.* Women may be *disadvantaged* by the prevailing management style, by entranched stereotypes about different forms of management.

(Young and Spencer, 1990)

The problem of sexual harassment, which was an issue in some way for a third of the women in the local government survey, is doubly complicated in the education service. Teachers face the possibility of harassment from both pupils and their colleagues, and (see Chapter 3) pupils also face the possibility of harassment from other pupils and staff. In an analysis of the impact of sexual harassment on the education service, De Lyon (1989) refers to a study carried out in Birmingham which indicated that 32 per cent of women secondary school teachers had experienced sexual harassment by colleagues and male pupils, 25 per cent by men only and 8 per cent by boys only.[6]

LEADERSHIP MODELS AND EDUCATIONAL CHANGE

Recent education research on leadership has tended to focus on the most effective models of leadership in managing the process of educational change and implementing new educational policies. In a case study of twelve schools in three school districts carried out in Canada in 1991, researchers focused on specific educational outcomes and the contributions of the principals of the schools to those outcomes. They examined how the principals interpreted the change process; the goals that they set; the long-term principals, values and assumptions; the constraints which they envisaged in relation to the change process; the solution process; and the feelings, mood and sense of self-confidence which the principals experienced in their problem-solving activities (Leithwood, Jantzi and Dart, 1991).

The Canadian researchers suggested that the principals in their study had approached their tasks of changing the organization in one of four ways: two they characterized as leadership (direct or indirect) and two as management (teacher-centred or building-centred).

- *Direct instructional leadership* corresponded to a pattern of systematic problem solving. It was an approach which was very 'hands on' and in which the principals demonstrated new instructional practices, coached teachers and ensured that second-order changes were made in the school to support implementation of the change process overall.
- *Indirect instructional leadership* included aspects of systematic problem solving. Principals using this pattern of problem solving were not as directly involved in classroom instruction as the direct leaders. However, it was a form of leadership which adapted well to larger organizations and 'multiple implementation responsibilities'.
- The researchers saw the term 'humanitarian' as capturing the focus of *teacher-centred management.* It was a form of leadership which placed the primary concern on the teachers' welfare, although there was little focus on classroom practices.
- *Building-centred management* focused on the routines and organization of the school, without any direct involvement in curriculum matters.

The researchers concluded that the two leadership models – direct and indirect instructional leadership – were the most effective modes of managing the educational change process. Principals who adopted either of these two leadership models interpreted the primary programme as a positive opportunity to meet student needs and were willing to take risks in pursuing their goals. Their attitude to change was characterized by enthusiasm and optimism and their strategy was one of involvement of parents and work colleagues. No major constraints were conceived and sophisticated problem-solving solutions were adopted to help staff through the change process. Student learning was cherished beyond all other values and teacher empowerment was seen as a necessary means to achieve that end (see Table 5.2).

Building-centred management was seen as the management style least suited to introducing change. Change was faced with resignation and viewed as a massive upheaval, with a lengthy list of constraints, particularly financial. It was very much a 'hands off' approach to administration and also one which had view goals related to students.

The researchers described their theory of leadership as *change through commitment*, which they linked to transformational leadership, a model of leadership that was interactive and based on negotiation. More specifically, transformational leadership

- identifies and articulates a vision;
- provides an appropriate model;

Table 5.2 Leadership models and change

| | Leadership | | Management | |
	Direct instructional	Indirect instructional	Teacher-centred	Building-centred
Interpretation of change	Complex problems Positive outcomes for pupil/clients	Complex but manageable problems	Massive upheaval	Accept initiative. Problem seen in terms of budget and
Goals	Focus on what is good for pupils/ clients/public	Wide-ranging, e.g. well-informed staff, outcomes for pupils, etc.	Slow down staff	No goals relating to pupils/clients/ public Goals to keep staff informed, allow time
Values	Outcomes for pupils/clients/ public – Take risks – Encourage participation and sharing	Although concerned about outcomes for pupils/clients/ public, particular focus on consequences for staff and *consequently* for pupils, etc.	Concern for staff	Order and serenity
Constraints	Constraints not impenetrable barriers to success	Staff who are not willing to change	Staff are moving too fast	Lengthy list. Great emphasis on financial constraint
Solution processes	Instructional strategies	Making sure staff understand issues	Depend on staff to supplement the process	'Hands-off' approach to administration Down to the staff Emphasis on money, release time
Mood	Excitement	Pleased about initiative	Pleased but uneasy	Resignation

Source: adapted from Leithwood, Jantzi and Dart (1991)

- fosters the acceptance of group goals;
- expresses high performance expectations;
- provides individualized support;
- provides intellectual stimulation.

(Based on Leithwood, Jantzi and Dart, 1991)

This notion of change through commitment fits well with the Rosener interactive leadership model described earlier. Interestingly, although gender had not been a primary research focus in the Canadian research, the researchers found that 4 of the 5 women in the study, but only 2 of the 7 men, were categorized as transformational leaders. The researchers were unable to conclude whether their findings were significant to gender or stemmed from the fact that the women principals came from the more successful of the three school districts in their study.

Undoubtedly, however, gender and gender expectations impact on management and leadership. Other research findings suggest, for example, that the gender of participants affects not only what is communicated but how it is communicated. Shakeshaft (1990), drawing on her research on educational administrators in the USA argued that there were significant differences between the management styles of female and male administrators. Such differences existed in a range of activities and assumptions of the administrators, and were manifested in a range of ways, including in the supervision patterns established by female and male administrators and in their expectations about their staff.

Shakeshaft suggested, for example, that male supervisors gave greater feedback to other men than to women and that, as a consequence, women did not get direct feedback from their male superiors. As a consequence women were denied the opportunity to hear criticism which would help them change their behaviour. According to Shakeshaft, male supervisors did not want to give critical feedback to women in case they cried, and frequently called on other women to tell their female supervisees that they were not doing a good job. The research showed, however, that men and women were equally likely to cry but that men cried only in front of other men, whilst women cried in front of either.

Particular difficulties arose for women when they became supervisors. Women supervisors were more likely to give feedback to women and men than were male supervisors. As this frequently was the first time that women supervisees had received critical feedback, female supervisors were often considered to be more critical than male supervisors.

Female and male administrators also had different expectations about their management teams and held different concepts of loyalty. Male administrators defined a loyal member of their management team as 'someone who will not disagree with me in public and will go along with my ideas'. If they dislike my ideas they will go and work for someone else. Women defined loyalty from their management team as 'doing the job well and speaking the truth'. Staff had a professional responsibility as loyal workers to show that there were other points of view. The expectation that women had about their management team was that staff would do the job competently and on time.

In a further piece of research on the hiring practices of male school administrators, Shakeshaft asked the interviewees whether they would consider hiring a 'traditionally attractive woman' in a job close to them. Although the majority of interviewees said that they would hire a woman for a post such as elementary school principal, few of the interviewees would consider hiring a woman for a post which required a close working relationship with them. Explanations for this behaviour (Shakeshaft, 1990) included:

- The school board wouldn't like it.
- My wife would be jealous.
- I don't know what I would do if I were attracted to her and wanted sex.

Shakeshaft concluded that there was male resistance to appointing women to certain senior education administrative positions which brought them into close daily proximity with the men because of male heterosexual expectations about sex and sexuality. She argued that issues about sexuality have to be confronted if sexual equality in the staffroom is to be achieved. Shakeshaft's analysis echoes some of the issues raised in Chapters 3 and 4. Expectations about sexuality, sexual harassment, and male power relations are all part of the uneasy and unspoken backcloth which lies behind the experience of many women staff and female students in our educational insitutions.

Other American research has focused on gender and leadership skills in education management. Fobbs (1990) examined the leadership styles adopted by women presidents of two-year public and private colleges. Seventy-six (84.4 per cent) of the 115 women presidents were included in her final research analysis. She examined whether the achievement styles of the women presidents fell into one of three domains: direct, instrumental and relational.

> The *direct domain* was characterized by the pursuit of activities designed to accomplish the tasks in hand through an approach which was often directly confrontational and competitive.

> The *instrumental domain* was characterized by activities that used personal accomplishments, or relationships, as 'conduits' to other achievements.

> Finally, the *relational domain* was characterized by activities which developed achievement by contributing to the tasks and goals of others.

The findings of the management theorists which Fobbs drew on for her analysis suggested that the achievement styles of the most successful managers were in the relational domain (Leavitt and Lipman-Blumen, 1980).

Fobbs found that the majority of the women college presidents (63 per cent) in her study were in the relational domain, 8 per cent in the instrumental, and 24 per cent in the direct domain. Within the relational domain the majority of women were characterized as collaboratively relational, i.e. preferring to work in groups and achieve in collaborative settings, and to share success and failure. The rest of the women whose leadership styles were in the relational domain were almost equally divided between *contributory relational* (meeting one's own needs for achievement by contributing to someone else's) and *vicarious relational* (identifying with others and feeling a winner when those close to you succeed). The concept of effective leadership in the relational domain is in accord with other concepts of leadership discussed in this chapter: transformational leadership, interactive leadership, situational leadership.

EDUCATIONAL LEADERSHIP AND SCHOOL PRACTICE

But what are the implications of these research findings for educational policy and practice? How do they relate to the central concern of the book with quality and equality?

Two central facts have emerged. The first is that managing for quality in a fast-moving educational service requires an adaptive leadership style which approaches change in a way that is positive for the organization and for the individuals within that organization. The second is that women are able to draw on a repertoire of styles and are inclined to adopt those styles which are most effective in managing the change process. Figure 5.2 summarizes the major elements in the research studies referred to in this chapter. According to Rosener, women tended to be transform-ational or interactive leaders but switched to being transactional leaders if co-operation would not work. According to Gerver and Hart, women drew on both masculine and feminine characteristics. All three studies, particularly that of Fobbs, identified the importance of collaborative activities in leadership. Fobbs's work suggested that the leadership styles of the majority of women college principals fell into this category. Similarly, Leithwood, Jantzi and Dart identified instructional leadership as the most successful model of leadership in managing significant educational change. It was a style more likely to be adopted by women than men.

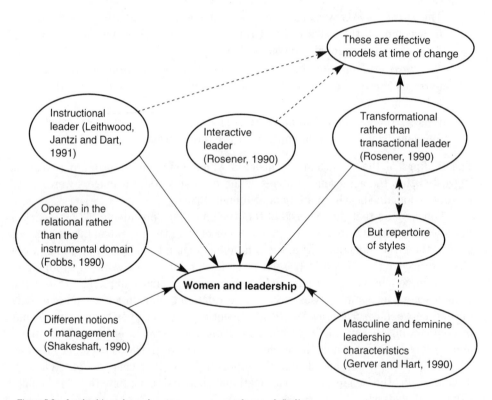

Figure 5.2   *Leadership styles and women: a summary of research findings*

In presenting this analysis about women and leadership, I do not seek to suggest that all women are good leaders and all men are bad leaders. The purpose of the analysis presented in this chapter has been to raise questions about the validity of the aggressive, finance-driven model of leadership that is emerging within the education system. Such a model is one which is more closely identified with men than with women and as such frequently excludes women from expectations about promotion, or opportunities for promotion. It also offers a limited vision of how the education service can be led and a narrow role model for students.

Through their socialization, women are more likely to adopt a co-operative, interactive form of leadership than men. But such a leadership model is, and can be, adopted by men. Freeing men from having to be competitive and allowing them the opportunity to be caring and involved and to use their intuition could have positive outcomes for women and men alike, and for the leadership of the education service. On the flip-side, women's capacities to take financial decisions need to be both acknowledged and developed. *The issue is not only one of recognizing and valuing women's leadership styles but also of fostering a new style of leadership in men.*

APPENDIX TO CHAPTER 5

In the late 1980s and early 1990s, central government has focused on management in the public sector, including the education service. Three particular national management initiatives have had an impact on management development in the education service: the Management Charter Initiative has focused on managerial competences; the School Management Task Force has promoted a drive towards effective management strategies; finally, the National Framework for Teacher Appraisal has been established, and from now on teachers will be appraised. All three initiatives have, however, largely ignored such issues as the under-representation of women and black and ethnic minorities in senior management, or the scope for the leaders of the education service to promote equality as well as quality.

The *Management Charter Initiative* was set up by central government to improve management standards in both the public and private sector. But it has focused on a narrow range of competencies, ignoring concepts such as the ability to read a situation, to form balanced judgements or to rely on intuition and political acumen (Cave and Wilkinson, 1991). By neglecting any consideration of the exercise of judgement, the MCI has failed to explore the discretion that managers have to influence decisions and outcomes.

The *School Management Task Force* was set up to improve management by reviewing the pattern of existing provision and supporting effective use of resources. It has concentrated on the broader pattern of provision and on those who are currently leaders, or are on the leadership track, excluding consideration of the pathways to leadership: whether some groups are more encouraged to be leaders than others. It assumes a level playing field in which all players have equal access to the game.

Teacher appraisal offers a structured and systematic opportunity to support and develop staff but could pose some problems for equality. Drawing on evidence from the United States, Al-Khalifa (1992) has suggested that male appraisers may be anxious about appraising women and unwilling to give critical feedback – an issue also raised by Shakeshaft (1990). Appraisers may also be insensitive to discrimination, or the problems of managing home and work. Appraisal offers the opportunity, however, to acknowledge the achievements of women – which they themselves frequently discount and which are discounted by others – and to identify their potential and promote their career development.

NOTES

1. Following this leak, the Commission for Racial Equality accused the government of lacking the political will to conclude its survey and publish the full findings.
2. The literature on education management often excludes consideration of such issues. A notable example of this is the book by Ribbins *et al.*, (1991), which otherwise provides a comprehensive review of contemporary issues in education management.
3. The appendix to this chapter briefly explores major government initiatives on management development and suggests that they have ignored equality issues.
4. This notion of situational leadership has been developed by a colleague, Judy White, in her work with chief officers in local government.
5. The findings stem from a workshop undertaken in March 1993 with women chief executives of local authorities. The workshop leaders were myself and Judy White. The workshop was the first stage in a research project, on women and leadership in local government, funded by the Local Government Management Board.
6. The survey was carried out by Brenda Addison and Elisabeth Al-Khalifa, in conjunction with the National Union of Teachers in Birmingham. Thirteen hundred questionnaires were distributed to teachers and 420 to college lecturers, of which 334 were returned by teachers (246 secondary and 88 primary) and 134 by college lecturers.

Chapter 6

Quality and equality: evaluating the context and the outcomes

INTRODUCTION

Goodwill alone will not produce quality, or equality, in schools. Chapter 3 illustrated how some teachers in mixed schools assumed that equality in coeducation was achieved merely by the presence of girls and boys in the same school and by registering girls and boys together, rather than in gender groups. Similarly, some teachers in girls' single-sex schools assumed that a single-sex environment automatically promoted girls' interests and furthered their educational and career prospects.

In pursuing quality in schools, one of the basic but fundamental problems has been that the agenda for change adopted by many schools has rarely been based on adequate information. Schools have simply not known what has been happening to pupils, other than at a general and aggregated level.

The UK government has set a national framework for measuring pupil performance which has largely excluded consideration of equality issues. The publication in national newspapers of league tables of performance – based on the scores gained in public examinations and Standard Assessment Tasks and soon to include measures of school attendance and pupil destination – has also ensured a focus on a narrow range of outcome measures.

The league tables of raw examination results are one useful source of information about pupil performance but they have their shortcomings. Firstly, the tables do not take into account the degree to which a school enables its pupils to overcome any social or educational disadvantage they have when they arrive at school: nor the extent to which those who are socially, or economically, advantaged benefit in their achievements from their school, rather than their home. That is, they do not take into account the 'value added' to the pupil by the process of schooling. Secondly, they add little to the debate about the quality of school experience. And finally, on their own they do not provide the information needed to ensure that school improvement takes place.

For improvement we need an understanding of both process and outcome: how do different groups of children experience schooling and what are the outcomes for them? As Chapter 4 demonstrated, such a double focus is likely to reveal significant differences between groups of children: girls and boys, black and white children. Sadly, the necessary information is rarely available on a systematic basis.

The information base about the employment opportunities and experiences of staff employed in our schools, or as education administrators, is even more deficient.

In the apparently liberated decade of the 1990s there is an assumption that women have achieved equal status and opportunities in the education workforce. Similar assumptions are made about black and ethnic minority staff, who are now deemed to be moving up the occupational ladder.

Such assumptions about the pattern of incremental change are not borne out by the existing evidence. The employment and promotional opportunities for women and black and ethnic minorities are limited. As was argued in Chapter 5, the pathways to leadership for women and black staff are still very different from those for white males. There is also some evidence to suggest that the business models and quasi-market arrangements that have arisen in response to recent legislation, and which now characterize many aspects of the education service, emphasize skills and attributes that are largely seen as male. Opportunities for women are not opening up but diminishing.

The purpose of this chapter is to suggest that we need a clear information base on staff and pupils and one that is linked to educational processes and outcomes. This would enable progress to be made on quality and equality. With these goals in mind, educators need two ask two initial questions:

- What are the processes and outcomes of schooling for different groups of pupils?
- What are the experiences and opportunities for their educational leaders?

The answers to these questions can be provided in a number of ways:

- through external inspection;
- through the school's own process of internal review, particularly through such activities as school development planning;
- through surveys of staff and profiles of student experience; and
- through systematic and focused attempts – by schools and the systems that support them – to look at both the context and outcomes of schooling.

This chapter focuses on quality and equality issues for pupils and staff through an examination of the resources, processes and outcomes of schooling. These issues are explored both within the context for evaluation and the measurement of performance set by central government and within the constraints and opportunities offered by systematic attempts to develop indicators of educational performance. The differing information needs of policy-makers, practitioners and users are examined and the chapter concludes by arguing for a national indicators framework which incorporates both quality and equality objectives.

MEASURING FOR QUALITY AND EQUALITY

The changes in the education system which have moved power and responsibility from local government to central government, and from central government of schools and institutions, place emphasis on the responsibility of individual schools and colleges to assess their own performance against criteria laid down by central government. Schools are also being called to account for their performance through the new inspection procedures carried out under the auspices of the Office for Standards in Education (OFSTED).

Little weight appears to have been attached by central government to the need for, or the capacity of, the local system to achieve management for quality. Besides, the government view of quality appears to exclude any consideration of equality. Despite this discouraging situation, there is still scope for educators at various levels of the system to make a positive contribution in this field.

Equality issues cut across all levels of the education system and are of fundamental concern for policy formulation. The Australian educators Ruby, Millan and Howe (1989) argue that although the research literature can provide information on trends in performance for girls and minorities compared with the general population on subject enrolment patterns by gender, and on the identification of stereotypes based on race and gender, yet this information is often fragmented and concentrates on proving disadvantage rather than providing a framework for monitoring progress towards equality. It is through monitoring progress towards equality that progress can be made.

> Indicators have the potential to push the symbolic goal of equality of outcome into the tangible reality of targets of achievement. They can do this by making stronger connections between policy goals, resource allocation, monitoring and evaluative procedures.
>
> (Ruby, Millan and Howe, 1989, p. 7)

But measuring for quality and equality is not a simple activity, requiring as it does an examination of resources, processes and environment, and outcomes of schooling.

Resources

The equality dimension is present at all levels of resource allocation in the education system, from access to pre-school provision to access to higher education and allocation of student awards.

> In 1987 there were almost 25,000 full-time undergraduates in the United Kingdom studying engineering and technology – only 2,741 of these were women.
>
> (Miles and Middleton, 1990)

For teachers and education managers, the equality dimension is manifested in areas such as the allocation of incentive allowances to teachers and the access to in-service training opportunities. Evidence from an NUT survey on teacher pay (Chapter 5) suggested that men have benefited from the arrangements for responsibility allowances created by the Teachers' Pay and Conditions Act 1987 (NUT, 1990).

Process and environment

As indicated in Chapters 2 and 3, pupils' learning experiences are highly differentiated by gender. The educational process and environment is influenced by the hidden curriculum – the messages which schools transmit to pupils through their underlying assumptions and the practices that result from these.

> When I was in the third year I went to play the drums and they wouldn't let me. They said it was a boy's instrument. It gave me the hump. Then when I wanted to do metalwork and woodwork they wouldn't let me.
> (Sally, aged 15)
>
> (Riley, 1985a)

Little attention has been given to the monitoring of process and environmental factors, yet there are particular hidden aspects of the school environment which can have profoundly negative consequences for some children and staff. Sexual harassment is one such factor.

Chapter 3 drew attention to a New York study which illustrated the extent and consequences of harassment on pupils (Shakeshaft and Cohan, 1990). Chapter 4 presented the findings from a Birmingham survey on sexual harassment of women teachers (De Lyon, 1989). The regular collection of such information not only draws attention to the extent and consequences of harassment but also provides a basis for challenging such practices. Such targeted information can help to create a climate and framework for change. Within the UK sensitive process information is often lacking at both local and national systems levels.

The process and environmental factors are linked for pupils and staff. A school climate in which girls are being harassed is one that is unlikely to be supportive to women staff. When male students hold prurient or stereotyped attitudes towards female students – and their views are not challenged – they are unlikely to esteem female staff as highly as male. Relationships between female and male staff are unlikely to be based on mutual esteem.

Some years ago I applied for a job as head of department in a boys' school. On a preliminary visit to the school the deputy headteacher told me that the boys tended to be a 'bit lippy about women' but I was not to take it too seriously, or personally. If things got out of hand, I could send the boys to him to be disciplined. I declined to go forward for interview for the job. This story illustrates the point that student–teacher interactions which reinforce male power relations create a professional environment which reduces the scope and range of opportunities open to women. Had I gone forward and been appointed to the post, I would have found myself in an environment in which I had to use the (male) power of senior colleagues to keep the boys under control. The climate was unlikely to have been one of mutual respect amongst colleagues and a common sense of purpose in challenging the stereotyped assumptions of the boys. Discomfort in the staffroom would have been reflected by conflict in the classroom.

An understanding of the impact of classroom processes – both from the viewpoint of students and staff – is vital to understanding and to changing outcomes.

Attempts to find out about the process of schooling require not only statistical information but also qualitative information about the processes. Teachers and pupils can provide this. They are connoisseurs of their own schools: their views and experiences deserve to be explored.

Outcomes

There are clearly gender-differentiated educational outcomes for pupils (in terms of subject and career choice) and for staff (in terms of job and promotional opportunities). To take one example from Chapter 5:

> Over the past decade, despite the increase in women in middle management, there has been a decrease in the percentage of women appointed as headteachers or deputies.
>
> (Migniuolo and De Lyon, 1989)

Although many studies have focused on aspects of gender disadvantage in education for pupils *or* for staff, the findings from these have rarely been aggregated at a national level and the information on pupils and staff has not been combined. We lack a comprehensive picture of disadvantage and an overall national framework for monitoring existing programmes, or evaluating the impact of future trends. What is required more urgently now than ever (Chapter 2), is a way of monitoring progress towards equality. Is there any possibility of achieving this within the framework that has been set up by central government?

BUILDING AN EDUCATIONAL EQUALITY DATABASE AND DEVELOPING EQUALITY INDICATORS

Background to the debate

Over the past decade there has been considerable focus in Britain on the measurement of performance in both the public and the private sector. Conservative administrations since 1979 have concentrated on the measurement of performance in the public sector as a way of increasing accountability to central government and ensuring that central government objectives are achieved.

Over the past five years or so, the extent and aspirations of evaluation have risen, resulting in an increase in scope for auditors (particularly the Audit Commission), inspectors (e.g. the new Social Service Inspection Unit) and for consultants who operate at the boundaries of government and provide a bridge between the values of the public and private sectors. For the most part evaluation has been developed to increase accountability and public control and to promote economic imperatives, rather than to support professional development (Henkel, 1991).

National governments have increasingly become concerned about indicators, both in relation to activities within their own countries and as a way of enhancing their capacity to make international comparisons and of assessing their economic competitiveness. In the late 1980s and early 1990s there have been systematic efforts to create international indicator systems designed to provide cross-national comparisons and to contribute to policy analysis. Such systems have been developed by the Organisation for Economic Co-operation and Development and by the European Community (Riley and Nuttall, 1994). Whether the framework is internationally or nationally prescribed, or more locally developed and tailored to specific local circumstances, I would argue that there is scope for analysis of performance on equality dimensions, such as race and gender.

The drive towards performance measurement in the UK has led to an 'epidemic of performance indicators in the Public Expenditure White Papers' (an increase from 500 in 1985 to 2,000 in 1988). These performance indicators have served as 'instruments of hands off managerial control and democratic accountability' (Carter, 1991).

The quest for performance indicators will continue into the 1990s, as central government increasingly regulates both public and private sector monopolies and as concerns about consumer satisfaction continue to grow (ibid.). Such a growth is already evident in local government. The Audit Commission, in response to the Citizen's Charter, has developed performance indicators for local government which local authorities are required to collect from 1 April 1993 and to publish in 1994. These indicators are intended to provide comparisons between authorities (on issues of cost, economy, efficiency and effectiveness) and inform customers and local residents about performance. More indicators are planned.

The Audit Commission has posed 77 questions, in a form supposedly representative of citizens' concerns. Nine of these questions are about education. Each question is linked to a number of specific indicators. The performance questions for education services are largely to do with the allocation of resources and include such information as costs per pupil and class sizes.

- How many children under five receive education?
- How much does it cost to educate the under-5s?
- How many places in schools are unfilled and how many over-filled?
- How many children have statements of special educational needs?
- How quickly are statements prepared?
- How many children are educated in special schools?
- How many students get discretionary rewards?
- How quickly are maintenance awards paid?
- How much is spent on schools?

(Audit Commission, 1993)

But the Audit Commission's general approach to the measurement of performance has largely ignored questions of equality. The 'citizens'' questions approach the issue of quality in a way that is blind to its implications for different groups of citizens. The Audit Commission does not ask who receives the limited nursery places, yet there is considerable evidence to suggest that access to under-5s provision has been influenced by issues of class and ethnicity, as well as issues of geography.[1]

The Audit Commission has taken a similarly narrow approach in a publication which analyses the outcomes and costs of educational courses for the 16–19 age group: a joint study with HMI (Audit Commission/OFSTED, 1993). The study examined the enrolment patterns and completion rates of young people in the full range of post-16 provision, drawing attention to high non-completion course rates in particular sectors. It recommended 'the development of quantitative techniques for measuring performance and costs', recognizing that such information could not 'capture all the aspects of the effectiveness of a course' (pp. 61–2). Such quantitative measures would include:

- statements of the proportion of students enrolled at the start of a course who achieve the intended qualifications, with the unsuccessful students broken down into those who did and those who did not complete the course;
- 'value-added' statements which relate students' achievements at the end of a course to their levels of achievement before they started.

(ibid., p. 62)

But the study ignored issues of differential access to courses for groups of students (female/male, black and white), or differential drop-out rates. Equality monitoring is not mentioned as an integral part of the process.

Both of these examples serve as reminders of the argument put forward in Chapter 1: that key stakeholders in the education system (in the two examples used here, local authorities and principals or heads of providing institutions for young people) can use their discretion to include the equality dimension, even when other agencies ignore it. Although local authorities are only required to publish aggregated information on the performance question set by the Audit Commission, they still have the scope to use the indicators exercise to highlight equality features such as:

- What access do female/male, black/white students have to discretionary awards?
- How many black/white children are educated in special schools?

Principals and heads of sixth-form colleges similarly have the scope to monitor for equality – and many of them are now doing this.

PERFORMANCE INDICATORS: 'DIALS OR TIN-OPENERS?'

Performance indicators have become part of the currency of public sector management. In reality, performance indicators are contestable notions, as a complex range of factors contribute to performance. Within this chapter on performance and evaluation in education, I prefer to use the term *education indicators* rather than *performance indicators* to denote the difficulties of developing measures of performance. The argument put forward is that education indicators are an important tool in assessing effectiveness, widening accountability and gaining understanding of the complexities of performance. But such indicators are not absolute measures of performance and need to be extended beyond narrow quantitative measures.

Education indicators are part of the search for information about educational outcomes and are thus part of an evaluative system. They are designed to strengthen monitoring and evaluation and provide accurate and comprehensive information, as a basis for effective policy-making, which ultimately will lead to improvement of educational outcomes. The belief underpinning the development of indicators is that the provision of such information will optimize the conditions for improvement.

Education indicators are measures of assessing the effectiveness or healthiness of schools, colleges, or education authorities. However, no one set of indicators will provide the judgement about whether a school or education system is effective.

To illustrate this point, Table 6.1 indicates the number of pupils suspended in different secondary-school divisions of the now defunct Inner London Education Authority (ILEA) between 1984 and 1988. The table shows a variation between the number of pupils suspended in the divisions: from 7.6 per 1,000 in Division 7 to 17.7 per 1,000 in Division 1, in 1987/88. The table also shows some variations on a year-by-year basis. In Division 2, for example, 205 pupils were suspended in 1987/88 compared with 150 in 1986/87 (ILEA, 1988).

Table 6.1 Number and rate of suspensions by division in the years from 1984/85 to 1987/88: secondary schools

Division	Number of suspensions				Annual rate of suspensions per 1,000 pupils			
	84/85	85/86	86/87	87/88	84/85	85/86	86/87	87/88
1	172	205	136	187	14.0*	17.7*	12.2*	17.7*
2	147	119	150	205	8.4*	6.9*	8.7	12.1
3	84	60	53	70	10.1	7.9*	7.4	10.1*
4	76	66	48	91	8.1*	7.5*	5.8*	11.6
5	114	105	51	116	10.9	10.2	5.0*	11.3
6	195	161	135	245	12.2	10.6	9.2	17.4*
7	141	115	72	89	9.9	8.7*	5.8*	7.6*
8	108	128	101	146	8.3*	10.7	9.2	14.5
9	146	162	130	126	16.5*	19.0*	16.4*	17.2*
10	141	152	153	175	9.4	11.5	12.6*	16.4*
ILEA	1,324	1,273	1,029	1,450	10.6	10.8	9.2	13.6

*Statistically significantly different from average rate for ILEA.
Source: ILEA (1988)

But are the figures provided in the table performance indicators? And if so, what do they demonstrate? On an area-by-area basis, are those divisions with the highest suspension rates those which are failing their pupils, or do the differences reflect socio-economic factors? If the figures were also presented on a school-by-school basis, what would be a successful school in the eyes of parents – one that suspended disruptive students, or one that kept them in school? Does a school with a relatively high suspension rate need help and support and possibly additional resources, or should it be penalized?

Breaking down the categories by groups of pupils might also indicate further complexities. As Table 6.2 illustrates, the ILEA information was also presented in a way that showed the proportion of pupils suspended from different ethnic groups: in 1987/88, secondary school pupils from Caribbean backgrounds were much more likely to be suspended than pupils from white European and Asian backgrounds.

Table 6.2 Percentage of boys and girls suspended from each ethnic group in 1987/88: secondary schools

	African	Caribbean	Ethinic Group Asian	Other black	White European	Other white
% of suspensions:						
Boys (N=976)†	3.6	29.3*	3.0*	4.9	55.9*	3.3
Girls (N=278)†	5.8	30.6*	1.4*	4.3	56.5*	1.4
Estimated % of secondary school population (1987):						
Boys	3.9	12.3	11.1	5.9	65.0	1.8
Girls	4.7	13.5	11.0	6.4	63.0	1.4

*Statistically significantly different from the corresponding proportion in the secondary school population.
†Excludes pupils for whom information on ethnic group was not available.
Source: ILEA (1988)

The information about suspensions presented in Tables 6.1 and 6.2 provides a useful indicator of student performance. It throws up a complex range of factors for further consideration and possible action and has a critical role to play in providing a fuller picture of children's experiences in schools. It is only through the collection and presentation of such information that hunches or assertions (such as those from black parents' groups in London that children of Caribbean backgrounds were more likely than other children to be suspended) can be verified.

But data on suspensions is no more the whole picture than data on examinations. The two need to be linked with a range of other information on performance, including pupils' own assessment of their schooling. It is through the regular and systematic linking of indicators that policy and practice can be changed.

To maximize its influence on policy and practice, information needs to be collected over time. The ILEA information on suspensions was collected over a number of years. Further information presented in the ILEA report but not included in this chapter showed that over a twelve-month period there had been a small decline in the number of pupils who were from Caribbean backgrounds suspended and an increase in those from white European backgrounds suspended. The implications of such shifts provide a focus for review and action from both policy-makers and practitioners.

The example of ILEA suspensions is used to illustrate the point that it is difficult to take one isolated indicator as an unequivocal measure of the effectiveness of a school. Education indicators cannot be seen as dials that provide clear and unambiguous measures of output. Instead education indicators can be more aptly described as 'tin-openers' which open up a can of worms and lead to further enquiry (Carter, 1989; Riley and Nuttall, 1994). If information about performance is properly collated, linked to other relevant data and presented in a clear and accessible way, it can provide an effective spur for action.

Education indicators, in providing information about education processes and outcomes, can enable schools, colleges and education authorities to:

- assess the effectiveness of their services;
- set themselves objectives;
- formulate target levels which relate to these objectives; and
- enable judgements to be made about progress in achieving those targets.

(Riley, 1990b)

THE PROBLEMS

Although there is agreement that education indicators are designed to give information about schools, or school systems, to policy-makers and practitioners, there is less agreement about the definition of an indicator, or the composition of an indicator system, or how far such information should be used to increase accountability. Parents now have public access to information about school examination performance, although this information is not broken down by race or gender. Indicators obviously provide important signals, but how and to what extent are such systems different from other information systems? How do they relate to inspection and self-evaluation? How are education indicators to be used: for policy analysis, for professional development, or for public accountability? (Riley, 1992a). These are all issues which need to be resolved by key stakeholders in the system such as: teachers, governors, policy-makers, parents and pupils themselves.

There is also considerable debate about what constitutes an effective education indicators system. Carter (1991), for example, has suggested that effective systems are typified by data sets which:

- are designed by the organization itself;
- provide information quickly on a relatively small range of indicators; and
- are linked to organizational objectives.

Such a framework emphasizes the importance of involving the stakeholders; and of devising a system which can be related to local purposes and linked to improvement.

Ruby, Millan and Howe (1989) have argued for the development of educational indicators which include an equality focus and which are based on the following criteria:

- provide valid information related to significant aspects of the education system;
- measure change over time and focus on enduring features of the system;
- are easily understandable;
- are problem-orientated;
- describe performance in terms of desired educational conditions and performance outcomes; and
- are feasible in terms of time, costs and expertise.

Potentially, this framework could also include the equality issues facing both pupils and staff and provide a focus for understanding the inter-relationship between the two in the process of teaching and learning. Both of these approaches, i.e. those of Carter and of Ruby *et al.*, are considerably different from the framework set by national government of examination and test results, school attendance and destination of school leavers.

PUTTING THE EQUALITY DIMENSION INTO QUALITY

Although education indicators provide the opportunity to develop a system which can monitor progress towards quality and equality, equality is frequently ignored when indicators are developed. Findings from a study of how ten local authorities approached the development of education indicators suggested that equality was largely a peripheral concern (Riley, 1992a). Examination performance was one of the few areas in which systematic attempts had been made to explore equality dimensions. Although most authorities had highlighted gender differences in examination performance, issues about ethnic monitoring had caused considerable difficulties in most authorities. However, one authority had used its annual Inspection Report (1989–90) to draw attention to the inadequacies of the information provided by schools and 'the striking [fact] that barely half the schools provided data on the ethnic origins of pupils in their returns of GCSE and A level results'.

Schools would be required to provide such information in the future. Overall, however, most authorities missed the opportunity to monitor equality and set equality goals, or to integrate equality into a broader quality framework. Yet education indicators can be linked to equality in a number of crucial ways:

- through the provision of a comprehensive database on race and gender;
- by providing opportunities to widen accountability to parents, students and the wider community on equality issues; and

- through linking the provision of such information to systematic monitoring over time and to targets of achievement.

Examination performance is one obvious example where the presentation of data by gender and ethnic origin can provide invaluable information (see Chapter 4). Table 6.3 gives the examination performance scores of Year 11 pupils in the Inner London Education Authority in 1987. (Scores were calculated by awarding 7 points for a grade A GCSE down to 1 for a grade G.) The table shows both gender and race differences. On gender, girls scored on average 4.2 points more than boys. But this average difference masks considerable variation: Pakistani girls and boys scored similar results, whilst 'other white European girls' scored 12.8 points higher than their male counterparts.

Table 6.3 Average performance scores of Year 11 students (ILEA, 1987)

Ethnic background	Males	Females
African	16.5	18.7
Arab	14.9	19.0
Bangladeshi	8.4	12.4
Caribbean	11.6	16.9
English, Scottish and Welsh	14.0	17.5
Greek	17.1	19.6
Indian	21.1	24.3
Irish	14.9	21.5
Pakistani	20.5	20.7
SE Asian	18.3	19.3
Turkish	12.1	14.3
Other black	13.1	18.8
Other white European	18.8	26.0
Other white	11.5	24.2
All	14.0	18.2

The table also shows considerable variation between pupils from different ethnic backgrounds, particularly amongst pupils from the Indian subcontinent, with girls and boys from Bangladesh scoring considerably lower than other Asian pupils. The table raises as many questions as it answers, such as how far these differences are related to social class, time spent in the UK or parental and teacher expectations.

Despite these complexities, such information is critical to policy-making and classroom practices. But even when such data have been collated, the presentation of information is also not without difficulties. An analysis of examination performance carried out by the ILEA in 1990 which showed that white children from England, Wales and Scotland were achieving lower examination scores than other children resulted in the following headlines in the London *Evening Standard* (9.3.90):

WE'RE THICKER THAN THE IRISH
Brit kids are dunces says exam survey

The results thus became major press headlines when they confounded the stereo-types.

CREATING AN EFFECTIVE INDICATORS BASE

There is considerable scope to develop education indicators which give a clear picture of the opportunities open to particular groups. Gilmartin (1980), for example, undertook a feasibility study of how a social indicator system could be constructed which could examine the status of women and minorities in education. The study traced the situation of women's unequal access to basic and higher education in the USA and identified the social factors which reduced women's opportunities at all levels. Gilmartin argued for the need to develop social indicators which would provide an overview of the status of girls and women and identified eight key policy dimensions for establishing such an indicator base:

- *Educational aspirations*
  What are the educational plans and expectations of pupils?
- *Enrolment*
  Among those qualified to enrol for a course, what proportion of female/male, black and ethnic minority students, enrol at successive educational stages (pre-school, post-school, adult, master's, doctorate)?
- *Retention and dropout rates*
  What are the dropout rates for each group, prior to completing each education stage?
- *Educational resources and school environment*
  What are the quantities and qualities of available resources and what are the characteristics of the school environment?
- *Educational achievements*
  What are the levels of educational achievement in terms of 'functional ability' in various areas (such as reading and mathematics) and also tested academic achievement?

Additionally, what are the broader educational benefits in terms of non-cognitive outcomes?

- *Subject matter*
  What subject matters are students taking and specializing in at the different levels?

Which of these subjects are likely to lead to employment with higher prestige and higher pay?

- *Employment as teachers*
  What proportion of college graduates become teachers?
      With how much training?
      At what levels?
      At what salaries?
      In what types of schools?
      With what sort of working environment?
- *Employment as education administrators*
  What proportion of college graduates become administrators at education institutions?
      How much training do they receive beyond college?
      What is their job level and salary?

Gilmartin argued that for each policy dimension the experience of female and male, black and ethnic minority, and white participants should be recorded. In order for such a system to be effective the variables would need to be measured over time and information collected on, for example, differences in enrolment rates for college courses, between female and male, black and white students. But the analysis would also need to go further, seeking to identify the *institutional barriers* that excluded women from higher education (such as stereotyping in counselling, course load, lack of child-care, educational resources and restricted school environment, unhelpful admissions practices). The *situational barriers* (e.g. lack of knowledge of educational opportunities, family opposition) would also need to be explored. Finally, there would need to be an examination of the *dispositional barriers* (e.g. the attitudes and expectations that affected the choices women made).

Gilmartin also argued that indicators should be developed in those areas in which educational intervention or non-intervention mattered. He suggested that for appropriate policy changes to take place a thorough analysis was needed of the implications of findings from each of the policy dimensions. He proposed a comprehensive framework which would provide information on a national systems level to help plan policies and resources. The framework could also be used at a local system and school level, to compare local performance and experiences and to develop appropriate activities which would improve educational experience, performance and opportunities.

Other attempts have been made to provide a systematic framework for measuring performance. Oakes (1989), for example, argued that past attempts in the USA to create indicators for monitoring the national educational system had concentrated on narrow outcomes, such as test scores. She argued that indicators which focused on the *context* of schooling were as necessary as those which focused on *outcomes*. Information about resources, policies, organizational structures and processes was essential to policy-makers if they were to understand the factors affecting education and make improvements.

> If policy-makers choose not to monitor context, they will fail to recognize that school characteristics mediate the effects of educational inputs (for

example, resources and state and local policies). They will also ignore how school characteristics can influence the classroom interactions that affect learning. Doing so, they will create monitoring systems that provide a superficial and simplistic portrayal of the performance of the educational system – one based entirely on results.

(Oakes, 1989, p. 183)

Oakes argued that a focus on context indicators would also enable policy-makers, parents and educators to be clearer about how effectively resources were being used, would restrain schools from emphasizing those 'outcome' indicators on which they looked good, and would provide policy-makers with important clues about why we get the outcomes we do. Such a framework was essential if schools themselves were to place any value on indicators and develop wider improvement programmes.

Context indicators could provide information about central features of the education system. Monitoring and observing these features would enable policy-makers to understand more about how the system works, how pupils experience the system and how results and outcomes are reached. It would also allow analysis to take place of any differences between groups of pupils who have had similar schooling experiences and generate clues about where improvement was needed and where it might be effective.

Oakes drew on the literature on the influence of school context (such as Coleman *et al.*, 1966; Goodlad, 1984) to focus on the process of teaching and learning. Essential to an understanding of these issues was an exploration of the inter-relationship between pupils and teachers. She posed four questions:

1 What school characteristics have clear links with highly valued educational experiences and outcomes?
2 What school-level indicators could help specify the central role of the school characteristics in the educational process?
3 What school-level indicators could press schools towards emphasizing the full range of desired educational experiences and results?
4 What school-level information might policy-makers and educators find useful for understanding schooling problems and shaping school improvement efforts?

From her review of the literature, she concluded that research had little to offer by way of answer to the first question, but could provide limited but useful information about the effects of specific school features on student outcomes, and thus give some answers to the other three questions. To progress these three questions she argued that classroom teaching and learning were influenced by three constructs which emphasized the central role of schools in the educational process and which offered fertile grounds for the development of indicators:

● *Access to knowledge:* the extent to which schools provided students with opportunities to learn knowledge and skills. (The focus of indicators in this area would be on the impact of the combined functions of school resources, structures and cultures. Indicators would look at issues such as access to courses and information, and equal learning time.)

- *Press for achievement:* the institutional pressure that the school exerts to get students to work hard and achieve. (In schools with strong pressure for achievement, both teachers and pupils take learning very seriously. The focus of indicators would be on the impact of different role models and assumptions, as well as organizational policies and strategies for parental involvement.)

- *Professional teaching conditions:* the conditions that can empower or constrain teachers and administrators as they are implementing teaching and learning programmes. (Indicators would need to look at those working conditions and opportunities which are most likely to attract and retain high-quality teachers and which impinge on classroom practices and pupils' levels of achievement. For teachers to be effective, they would need a degree of autonomy and flexibility. Motivation would be a key indicator.)

Oakes suggested that the three constructs – access to knowledge, press for achievement and professional teaching conditions – served to emphasize the central role of schools in the educational process. Schools were 'mediators of resources' through concrete decisions about how to distribute resources, or how to determine the norms, relationships and structures in a school. An examination of the three constructs enabled a focus on resources in a wider frame and an understanding of their connection with beliefs, values and expectations.

The contextual factors identified by Oakes were *enablers* of pupil learning, rather than *causes*. The challenge in the UK is to develop education indicators which schools can use to review the progress and experience of individual children and groups of children and set these alongside the experience of the staff themselves. Indicators also need to provide a basis of information through which schools could be called to account for their performance – in ways that make sense to parents and local communities – and which also reflect the social and economic context of the schools themselves.

EDUCATION INDICATORS: NATIONAL AND LOCAL PURPOSES

National and local governments and schools themselves have different purposes in collecting and using education indicators. There are obvious tensions in providing education indicators for the various groups that use them: policy-makers (politicians and managers), providers (teachers) and users (parents and children). Policy-makers at all levels require indicators which do justice to the complexities of the system. Teachers require indicators which are user-friendly and which provide information about the overall performance of a school and of individual departments, or parts of a school (infant/junior). Parents and children need clear and accessible information that reflects their concerns and priorities.

The needs and requirements of policy-makers at the different layers in the system are also different. Local governments require information about the trends within their locality, so that they can ensure that appropriate support and training is supplied. National governments require information about educational standards and national trends. (The UK government has specifically required schools to publish information about examination performance, in order to increase parental choice.) National governments also require information about international trends, both as a reference point and also as a way of redirecting national efforts.

At all of these levels, equality dimensions can play their part. At the international level, the OECD has produced comparative indicators for 22 OECD countries. These indicators (which have been developed through the INES project on international education indicators) have focused on issues such as: spending on education; participation rates; pupil–teacher ratios; the number of scientists produced (OECD, 1992). Although there have been considerable technical and organizational problems in collecting this data (as countries collect data in ways that reflect the needs of their own systems), nevertheless the OECD framework is potentially a powerful source of comparison on equality dimensions. It provides the opportunity to ask such questions as: how do participation rates vary by gender, or race? What are the policy implications of any differences for the allocation of future educational resources, or access to the labour market?

At national levels, governments have the opportunity to develop indicators to reflect a range of national purposes and goals. The US government has attempted to do this through *Education Counts* (1991), which is described as 'an education indicators system to monitor the nation's educational health.' *Education Counts* makes explicit national goals and the strategies which are being adopted to measure those goals. It articulates a strong valuation of the role and contribution of teachers and focuses on the status of children and their families, making clear the tie between poverty and educational disadvantage. One of its most explicit objectives is to put equality issues on the agenda.

Education Counts suggests that education indicators should be based in three areas:

- *learning:* learner outcomes and the quality of educational institutions;
- *social context:* students' readiness for schools and the degree of societal support for learning; and
- *national values and aspirations:* for the economy and for a more equitable society.

This challenges the *input* (resources) – *output* (examination results) model, which is increasingly dominant in the UK, and provides a broader context for measuring achievement. It offers the potential of a national framework which strives for both quality and equality objectives – a framework which is currently absent in the UK.

Education Counts is in many ways an uplifting report. However, it leaves unanswered such fundamental questions as:

- Can an education system be moved on through public accountability and reporting?
- How can the education values asserted in the report become shared values within the system?

For improvement to take place, there has to be a clear link between systems which measure performance and activities aimed at sustaining improvement. It may be easier to test and measure than to improve.

In England and Wales, central government has prescribed certain national goals through the National Curriculum and testing and through the publication of information about performance on national tests and examination results. At the same time, however, it has severely weakened the capacity of the local system (local authorities) to sustain and improve quality by withdrawing substantial local resources for quality monitoring and curtailing the responsibilities of local authorities for their local educational services in a significant number of ways (see Chapter 2).

USING EDUCATION INDICATORS AT THE LOCAL LEVEL TO IMPROVE QUALITY

The future and role of local authorities in the provision of local education services remains uncertain. Many commentators have argued that local authorities no longer have a role in sustaining and improving quality. Whilst I would argue that local authorities still have a role to play in sustaining and evaluating quality, given the constraints imposed upon them and the limitations of their resources they need to be very clear about the nature of their new quality role. Education indicators – and in particular those that take on the two dimensions of quality and equality – can make a useful contribution to that new role. Local authorities have the scope to link education indicators to other methods of assessing institutional effectiveness and, even more importantly, to create a synthesis between different forms of evaluation and schemes for school improvement.

There are three particular ways that local authorities can use education indicators to sustain quality through a *learning focus*, an *accountability focus* and a *change focus*.[2]

The *learning focus* stems from the ability of local authorities to combine their intelligence and information systems with information gained about school per-formance through inspection and thus provide schools with the tools to evaluate their own performance. It is an activity which also draws on research, such as that on school effectiveness, which refutes past claims that school activities cannot override the effects of social and economic background factors, and research projects from within the authorities themselves – although these are increasingly limited by the squeeze on local authority resources.

The *accountability focus* sees accountability for performance as being shared between the school and the local authority, and endeavours to translate information about performance into a wider public arena. Education indicators – which take into account the views of producers and consumers of the education service – are a key element in the accountability focus.

The *change focus* recognizes the instrumental role of the local authority in supporting schools in adapting to change. It sustains this through an integrated approach which links a comprehensive programme of in-service training, to direct support to schools: working with them to identify not only the characteristics of good or successful schools but strategies to achieve success. It is a focus which draws on the traditions of school self-development and reinforces the notion of the school as the primary actor and unit of improvement.

Promoting quality in this way is an interactive and developmental process which can only be sustained at a local level. Central government can prescribe quality goals but it cannot ensure quality outcomes. Local authorities are uniquely positioned to contribute to quality and support school effectiveness.

At all of the three levels described, equality is an integral issue. Earlier in the chapter it was suggested that local authorities could ensure that their answers to the performance questions set by the Audit Commission included equality issues. The questions that need to be asked are, for instance:

- How are different groups of pupils (girls/boys, black/white) best served by the education opportunities made available to them?
- Is this information made clear to parents through accountability systems?
- What change strategies are being adopted to meet the needs of different groups of children?

Local authorities also have the scope to develop education indicators which reflect the equality dimensions for staff and which look at the inter-relationship of the experiences of staff and pupils.

It is critical that schools are involved in the development of such indicators and receive usable information about outcomes. But given resource constraints, such indicators cannot be developed at the school level alone. Schools also need to be drawn outside their limited boundaries into a wider comparative frame and be held accountable for the performance of their pupils and for the employment opportunities offered to staff.

In establishing a framework for education indicators, local authorities would need to develop indicators at three levels in their organization (Riley, 1992c):

- *LEA service indicators:* to evaluate the effectiveness of the central services provided to schools and institutions. Indicators could focus, for example, on resource issues such as the gender differences in the provision of in-service training to staff, or allocation of discretionary awards to students.
- *LEA-wide institution indicators:* these would focus on key elements of the service provided by schools and institutions. Indicators could be used to provide comparative gender information about the promotional prospects of staff, or the career choice of pupils.

123

● *Institution-derived indicators:* these would reflect the objectives of individual schools and institutions. Indicators could assess the effectiveness of individual schools in meeting the aspirations of both female pupils and staff.

If parents and governors and pupils themselves are to have a real say in education, then a much wider span of information than examination results is needed to judge school effectiveness. A way of engaging all the partners in education is to develop both quantitative and qualitative education indicators which reflect the experience of all pupils. Qualitative indicators could draw on information derived from interviews and surveys. The education indicators would need to focus on both aggregated information about all pupils and also information to show the comparative experiences of different groups of pupils, such as girls and boys. The education indicators would be used to assess the effectiveness of schools, colleges and local education authorities in the achievement of equality goals and to set new targets for achievement.

The scope therefore exists for local authorities to use education indicators at the local level to improve quality. This role, which can only be achieved with the co-operation of schools, enables the local authority to act as a bridge between local purposes and national goals. As is illustrated in Figure 6.1, local authority endeavours can coalesce around four activities: data interpretation, data presentation, qualitative reflection and a refocus on new goals. Data collection underpins these activities.

Data interpretation is the ability to interpret both international data on educational performance (such as the INES project – see p. 121) and national data on the employment of staff in education. An essential element of this interpretative process is also the ability to analyse the plethora of data collected through different local authority functions and services such as social services and planning, and to make this meaningful to educational concerns. The equality aspects of all such information need to be included in the analysis.

Data presentation is the ability to present information in clear and accessible forms, making it user-friendly for parents, teachers and governors. Such information has to draw from a number of sources and include indicators which evaluate both the education context and the outcomes of schooling. It also has to be presented in ways which will enable schools to measure their overall progress and the progress of groups of pupils over time.

Qualitative reflection is a critical part of the whole process. Local authorities have to work in partnership with schools to understand what is happening in schools and to reach some measure of agreement about how quality can be assessed, monitored and improved. Figure 6.1 shows a two-way arrow between the local authority and the school, on qualitative reflection, indicating the interactive nature of the process.

An essential aspect of the process of qualitative reflection is that it includes the views of the participants themselves: parents, pupils and teachers. Such reflections will enable both the schools themselves and the local authority to explore qualitative

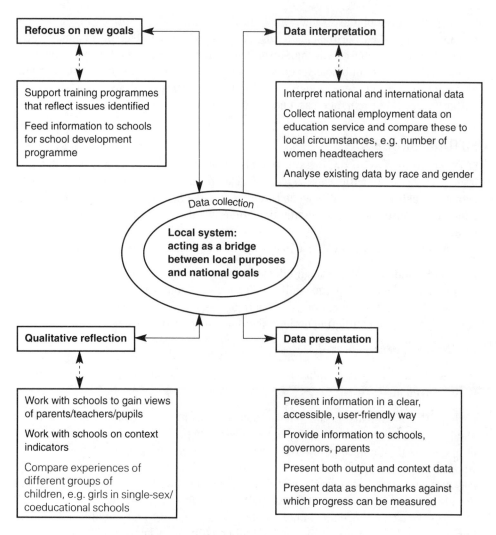

Figure 6.1 *Using education indicators at the local level to improve quality*

differences in the educational experience of groups of children and to address such questions as: how does the educational experience of girls in single-sex secondary schools compare to that of girls in coeducational schools? Are the differences as striking as those found in the HMI survey referred to in Chapter 3 (p. 41), on how schools prepared girls for adult and working life (DFE, 1992), or as in the research findings in Chapter 4?

For the fourth activity, *refocus on new goals*, the partnership between schools and the local authority needs to continue if education indicators are to be more than a paper exercise and to have some link with phased improvement. Data interpretation, data presentation and qualitative reflections all need to feed into the change and refocusing process through in-service training and school development programmes.

As the development of such an indicator framework is both costly and time-consuming, local authorities need to plan and prioritize. The development of a comprehensive database is a long-term goal which can be achieved by developing education indicators in blocks, each with a particular focus. Such an approach would allow for a phased development. The database established by local education authorities could be expanded as a national database.

FUTURE ISSUES

The opportunity exists in Britain and elsewhere to monitor quality and equality issues in the systematic way suggested. The purpose of doing this would be to establish quality and equality goals throughout the education service and to change educational outcomes for students and professional opportunities in education for staff.

A number of key issues arise in developing such an approach:

- Should schools (or local education authorities) be rewarded for their achievement of quality and equality goals, or penalized for failure?
- How can the education consumers be engaged in the debate and what happens if conflicting notions about equal opportunities emerge?

But the fundamental question is:

- What will push equality issues for pupils and staff on to the national agenda?

Perhaps the answer lies in the debate about increasing the accountability of schools and local education authorities for the services they provide and for the performance of pupils. As public accountability increases, it will become more publicly apparent who is failing and who is succeeding in our education system. Public accountability may also serve to clarify how the quasi-market arrangements introduced over the last decade or so have contributed to these patterns of success or failure.

The heart of the educational matter is that quality and equality for female pupils cannot be separated from quality and equality for women staff. Those who are unimpressed with the merits of the case for staff may be persuaded to tackle inequality in the staffroom in order to ensure that pupils experience equality in the classroom.

NOTES

1. For a fuller discussion of these issues see Penn and Riley (1992).
2. This framework draws on Coleman and Larocque (1990).

Chapter 7

Quality and equality – and the pursuit of common objectives

BRINGING EQUALITY BACK INTO THE QUALITY DEBATE

What constitutes a quality education service has been, and will continue to be, an issue for debate and dispute amongst politicians, professionals and the public. Questions also remain unanswered about how quality can be assessed: by quantitative performance standards, or by qualitative measures which reflect less tangible outcomes.

Whilst over the past 50 years politicians and professionals have disagreed about what constitutes quality outcomes, lack of quality has been commonly defined as the wastage of the ability of some children. Definitions of who those children are have, however, varied.

Proponents of the 1944 Education Act envisaged a meritocratic and differentiated system in which all children would be educated to their age, aptitude or ability and which would provide an upward route for bright working-class children to join their middle-class peers. In the 1960s advocates of comprehensive education argued for an undifferentiated education experience as the only way to challenge class bias and inequalities and end the wastage of working-class talent. In the 1970s and early 1980s elements of gender and race equality were tacked on to this predominantly class initiative. Champions of the 1988 Act sought to make a reality of consumer choice and to restore notions of merit: excellence through worth.

Common to each of these different phases was tension brought about by competing priorities, limitations of resources, and conflict between policy-makers and practitioners and between central and local government. What has dogged the footsteps of those leading the education vanguard at each of these successive stages over the past 50 years has been their inability to build on any strengths from the previous phase, or to acknowledge the complexities of a child's school experience.

Advocates of comprehensive education, in their determination to provide an undifferentiated school experience that would challenge class inequalities, were initially blind to inequalities of race and gender. Advocates of the new meritocracy seem similarly oblivious to issues of equality, called by Willetts (1992) the key anti-Conservative concept. According to Willetts (Member of Parliament and past Director of the Conservative 'think-tank', the Centre for Policy Studies), whilst the new Conservatism supports equality in areas such as voting, juries and legal processes, it views support for other aspects of equality as not only wrong in principle but muddled in practice. Equality and egalitarianism, in his view, are now unfortunate and 'seductive' remnants of socialism which must be eradicated:

> There is one key idea, seductive and with a strong emotional appeal
> which cannot be absorbed into conservative thought: egalitarianism.
>
> (Willetts, 1992, p. 109)

According to this analysis, the fundamental weakness of egalitarian policies is that they do not increase opportunities. But this is not necessarily the case in education. Equality policies can open up opportunities to disadvantaged groups that are not advantageous to them but to the rest of society. It is in this sense that meritocratic notions of quality can be linked to equality.

In order to achieve meritocratic goals – excellence through worth – obstacles to the achievement of those goals must be removed. What this book has argued is that the lack of equality of opportunity within the education system is a systematic obstacle to girls and women achieving their full potential. Quality and equality may be competing objectives but they can also be complementary objectives. The pursuit of equality is one route to quality.

Inevitably, as has been demonstrated throughout the book, there are tensions between the two objectives. Quality for one group of users or providers of the education service may not be the same as quality for another group – which is not to say that there are no absolute quality standards. Those who are making decisions about the allocation of resources or the nature of the organizational arrangements in schools have to decide on competing priorities; how to challenge past practices; and how to review both processes and outcomes.

A SUMMARY OF THEMES

The educational landscape has changed beyond recognition over the last decade. The power, authority and influence of individuals and organizations within that landscape have also changed (see Chapter 2). Local education authorities still retain some responsibility for the planning, organization and support of local education services. But powers have shifted from local authorities, not only to central government but also to a range of non-elected funding councils and to schools and governing bodies. How each of these new and existing organizations – and the individuals in them – will exercise their power and influence as yet remains unclear.

What is clear, however, is that those involved in supporting and delivering education services have considerable scope to influence both quality and equality outcomes through the exercise of their discretion. Chapter 1 suggested that the notion of *discretion* was a key concept in education management. It described the exercise of discretion as a quintessentially human activity which acts as a bridge between facts and values in decision-making.

How this discretion was exercised – or not exercised – in the pursuit of equality goals was a fundamental concern of Chapters 3 and 4. Both chapters illustrated how the boundaries for action are different for policy-makers and practitioners. Yet both groups can have significant impact on the allocation of education resources, on processes and on outcomes. Each has the discretion to ignore inequalities, or to contribute to the provision of equal education experiences. Without action, however, the structural inequalities created by history – of race, class, or gender – will remain unchallenged.

The book has also tried to demonstrate that the quality–equality conundrum for pupils is not separate from, but integral to, quality–equality issues for staff: classroom and staffroom issues merge and overlap. Girls' unequal access to classroom time and playground space is mirrored by women's unequal access to positions of leadership within the education service. Girls concentrate on their school work and developing good relationships with their peers. Female teachers concentrate on the daily business of keeping a school running and developing effective working relationships between teachers and pupils. But, as Chapter 5 demonstrated, women also have the capacity to offer the kinds of educational leadership needed in a time of change and uncertainty. Action by government, by local authorities and by governing bodies to remove the obstacles to women's promotion could release a reservoir of talent which could be harnessed to make the educational improvements that are our national goals. Yet again equality strategies could be used to achieve quality objectives.

Information about the education performance of children and the employment opportunities of staff is the essential starting point for change and improvement. Central government has been right to make the provision of information about performance a central issue and to insist that professionals are accountable to parents. In the past schools have simply not known how well their pupils were doing. But official league tables are only a part of the answer. They provide limited information about the processes, experiences and outcomes of schooling for different groups of pupils. They have nothing to say about the opportunities and experiences of their educational leaders. These issues must be priorities for the future.

SOME POLICY IMPLICATIONS

National government

At all levels of the education service there is scope to promote the development of quality and equality. Central government has significant powers to influence quality and equality for students through the general goals and framework which it sets – in areas such as the National Curriculum, or teacher training. But central government currently operates a narrow definition of quality – one that has largely excluded consideration of equality issues.

A similar parsimony is seen in the government's approach to staff issues. Here initiatives have gone little beyond support for Opportunity 2000, a scheme designed to encourage firms to take action to improve opportunities for women – an initiative which may have lost the active support of the CBI.[1] But many other European governments have themselves developed specific initiatives to enhance opportunities for women and acclaim their skills and contribution to the education service.

In Norway, Sweden and the Netherlands a range of programmes have been developed and supported by the various governments. Sweden has a national leadership programme with a particular focus on women and has also set national targets for improvement: the two together have had significant impact on the promotional opportunities for women at middle and senior management levels in education (Nylen and Sorhuus, 1990). The Netherlands has undertaken a similar affirmative action programme aimed at bringing women into education management. The project, which is part-funded by the Ministry of Social Affairs and Employment, is targeted at school boards and managers and promoted through seminars and conferences. It supports a package of programmes, including action on recruitment, career support and the provision of child-care (Netherlands Centre for School Improvement, 1990).

Although, as Chapter 5 suggested, women are under-represented in positions of educational leadership in many OECD and developing countries, there is growing evidence to suggest that with strong national leadership the situation can be radically changed. In Norway, for example, the percentage of women headteachers in primary and secondary schools has tripled over the last ten years from 8 per cent to 28 per cent. Legislative changes in Norway such as the Equal Status Act, which offers preferential treatment to female students in post-compulsory and higher education, have helped to create the climate for change. The Norwegian Ministry of Education has also promoted the advancement of women through specific management development programmes and through the integration of equality issues into its educational leadership programme (Pettersen, 1990). The Dutch Ministry of Education is similarly undertaking an affirmative action programme which includes opportunities for management training and a policy of ensuring that women candidates are considered for managerial vacancies in state schools (Netherlands Centre for School Improvement, 1990).

Local government

The opportunities for local authorities to influence educational processes and outcomes are the product of legislative, financial, political and bureaucratic factors. As was outlined in Chapter 2, the current education powers and responsibilities of local authorities are determined by a statutory framework to provide specific services – a framework which has become more nationally prescriptive over the last decade – and by a discretionary framework which relates to the level and provision of non-statutory services. Financial changes have brought about a reduction in many of these discretionary educational services, such as music, swimming, adult and youth services.

Through national controls on funding, a new version of equity is emerging which is based on treating all children – with few exceptions – the same: that is, providing them with the same level of funding regardless of need. There is a contradiction, however, between this notion of parity through equal funding and the unequal levels of funding local authority maintained schools compared with city technology colleges or grant-maintained schools. The latter received a capital grant of £231 per pupil, compared with £109 for pupils in local authority maintained schools, plus a one-off transitional grant of £60,000 (1991/2 figures).

Despite these funding contradictions, there are still opportunities for local politicians to exercise their discretion through resource and organizational decisions which reflect the different purposes and priorities of their own local authority and its communities. The decisions that local authorities make reflect different values and assumptions and have implications for different groups. Through exercising their discretion, local politicians have the power to decide whose needs are legitimate. By exercising their discretion in relation to equal opportunities, politicans can affect outcomes for particular groups: through provision for training courses for women returning to employment; through special mother-tongue teaching classes for new immigrants; or through measures to support children with special needs into mainstream schools.

A local authority can also exercise its discretion through its bureaucratic practices: the decisions that officers make about the organization and running of services. Such decisions could include, for instance, whether a crèche service is provided at an adult education institute, whether information about a course has been translated into various languages and whether there is disabled access or loop-hearing facilities.

But there are many other areas in which the local authority can demonstrate its educational leadership and exercise its discretion: in supporting strategies which promote the integration of quality and equality objectives; in developing and supporting appropriate in-service courses and management development; in working with schools to identify the needs of the various groups of children within the school community; or in supporting the training and developmental needs of school governors. As Chapter 6 suggested, developing performance measures which will enable schools to come to grips with the effect of their policies and practices on children and linking such information to effective strategies for school improvement is still an area in which local authorities can be influential. One of the many unresolved issues for the future is who will provide such a service for grant-maintained schools.

Schools and colleges

Chapters 3 and 4 demonstrated how the interactions, the assumptions and the expectations of those involved in the day-to-day delivery or support of education services can affect both processes and outcomes. There are still major unresolved issues about girls' restricted educational experience in coeducational schools and the limitations of career advice and post-school education and training. But such issues can be challenged by vision and leadership at the top (by headteachers such as Miss C, described in Chapter 4) and through the commitment and awareness of classroom teachers. The initial training of teachers and appropriate in-service training and support for change activities in school are also critical for the development of quality and equality. Schools and colleges also need to take on board the management development needs of their staff. As Chapter 5 suggested, staff appraisal can either open up new opportunities for staff or reinforce stereotypical assumptions.

Women and management

Chapter 5 highlighted some of the obstacles which women face in becoming education leaders but also the richness of experience and styles which women can bring to such positions. But if women are less confident about their skills and readiness for promotion, as the research suggests (Ouston, Gold and Gosling, 1992), then action is required to ensure that women's skills and expertise are acknowledged, particularly in middle management.

Women often reach middle management positions, particularly in schools, but it has been suggested that this often locates them in an 'in-between domain' with unclear tasks and responsibilities and where they may feel caught between the needs of their own team (departmental or year group) and the demands of the school management team. For many women being in middle management is comparable to being in the middle of an hourglass – a very visible and vulnerable position, which leaves them open to both praise and resentment (Schuijt, 1990).

Schuijt identified two obstacles for women in moving from middle to senior management. The first was that although women performed many leadership and managerial tasks, such as exercising negotiation skills, managing human resources, team building, introducing educational innovation, coaching people through the change process and managing conflict, they did not label these tasks as management or leadership, or identify the qualities which they had to perform those tasks. Women themselves failed to acclaim their leadership qualities. Professional development programmes are an important ingredient in creating opportunities for women by extending the repertoire of skills and knowledge available to them.[2]

Schools and governing bodies

Schools and governing bodies now have much greater powers to influence the agenda for pupils and to decide who should be employed within the school. These new powers and responsibilities could create or could restrict opportunities. As was suggested in Chapter 5, the evidence to date is that women are losing out in the new business-orientated education world. Appointing bodies need to recognize that people-orientated skills and the ability to negotiate and develop open communication with staff and pupils are vital ingredients to successful management. Local authorities can do much to support schools in their recruitment and employment policies and schools and colleges themselves can also take the initiative to set a new agenda for equality.

Milton Keynes College, for example, developed an initiative which it described as 'total equality management', the purpose of which was to enable women and men to overcome any barriers to their recruitment and promotion. The structure of the organization, the systems for decision-making, the skills and attitude of the staff, and the organizational style were examined. The college review identified the hierarchical structure of the department and came up with proposals for a new structure which reduced the number of senior management posts from 7 to 4 and created 17 new middle management posts. The creation of these new posts opened a wider range of career opportunities. The development of a comprehensive management development programme (with opportunities for both women and men) and targeted press advertising for the new posts succeeded in radically altering the staffing structure of the organization (see Table 7.1).

Table 7.1 Milton Keynes College: impact of total equality management on staffing structures

| | 1986 | | 1990 | | |
	F(121)	M(119)	F(166)	M(134)	
Senior managers	1	6	2	2	full-time
Middle managers	0	13	18	12	full-time
Lecturing and support staff	50	70	56	48	full-time
Lecturing and support staff	70	30	90	72	part-time
Total		240		300	

Source: Dicketts and Limb (1991)

CONCLUDING THOUGHTS

During my visit to Marchbank school (see Chapter 4), I had asked the girls what changes they would want to see if I returned to the school in ten years' time: 'No racism, no sexism, equal rights ... It should be how the world should be.' Their comments made me look to the future and speculate on what I might find if I returned to Marchbank, or a similar school, in the year 2003. How would I know whether that school provided quality and equality for its pupils and staff?

One indication of quality in its broadest sense would be that equality would no longer be an issue for pupils, staff or parents. Girls' football would be as normal an activity as boys' football. Girls would not be excluded from classroom activities by the rowdy behaviour of boys. But the changes that would have taken place for that school to achieve quality and equality would have been ones that would have included both the boys and the girls. Learning to co-operate, share and work together would have enhanced opportunities for boys, as well as for girls. Those boys who are currently alienated from school and achieving poor examination results would have been given new opportunities. Schools would have learned to deal with the disaffection of boys – particularly of black boys.

A second indicator of a quality educational experience for all pupils would be that pupils, parents and teachers would be in agreement that that was the case. I might glance at the league table of examination results, but I suspect that the real answer to my question would come from all the users and producers of the school's services.

If I then wanted to explore how the school had achieved quality, I suspect that I would discover that it had developed a clear vision of what it was trying to achieve and operated a strategy along the following lines:

> If we regard pupils as the workforce and the teachers as the managers, we can then apply principles advocated by Deming and others to improve quality, by giving greater responsibility to the pupil for the quality of their work. Until pupils are invited to share in deciding the ways in which quality is to be achieved, they will continue to act for much of the time

like recalcitrant workers, particularly in secondary schools, where they are at present subject to all the controls and checks which characterized an old-fashioned and inefficient production line.

(Hutchinson, 1993)

One of the lessons that I have learnt from interviewing pupils over the past ten years is that they are capable of providing fair and critical assessments of their school experience. They are also capable, in partnership with their parents and teachers, in helping us along the yellow brick road to quality and equality.

NOTES

1. See note 1, Chapter 1.
2. For example, the University of Manitoba, Winnipeg, has developed a leadership programme (the AHEAD course) aimed at women in higher-education institutions who wish to assume senior administrative roles. The course explores the culture and behaviour of academic institutions and examines issues around organizational leadership and the development of interpersonal relationships in order to enhance both individual and organizational goals and professional development (Mays, 1990).

Bibliography

Alban Metcalfe, B. N. and Nicholson, N. (1984) *The Career Development of British Managers*. London: British Institute of Management Foundation.

Al-Khalifa, E. and Widdowson Migniuolo, F. (1990) Messages for management: the experience of women's training. Paper presented to the conference on Equal Advances in Education Management, Vienna, 3–6 December.

Al-Khalifa, E. (1992) Appraisal. In Myers, K. (ed.), *GenderWatch, After the Education Reform Act*. Cambridge: Cambridge University Press.

American Association of University Women (1992) *How Schools Shortchange Girls*. Report commissioned by the AAUW and researched by the Wellesley College Centre for Research on Women.

Anthias, F. and Yuval Davis, N. (1983) Contextualising feminism – gender, ethnic and class divisions. *Feminist Review* **15**, Winter, 62–75.

Arnot, M. (1986) Sex discrimination and educational change, *Module 4: Race, Gender and Education Policy-making* (Open University, E333). Milton Keynes: Open University Press.

Arnot, M. (1989) A crisis or a challenge? Equal opportunities and the national curriculum *NUT Education Review* **3**(2), 7–13.

Arnot, M. (1991) Equality and democracy: a decade of struggle over education, *British Journal of Sociology of Education* **12**(4), 447–67.

Association of University Teachers (1993) *Update* (8) (June).

Audit Commission (1993) *Citizen's Charter Indicators: Charting a Course*, Audit Commission for Local Authorities and the National Health Service in England and Wales. London: HMSO.

Audit Commission and the Office for Standards in Education (1993) *Unfinished Business: Full-time Educational Courses for 16–19 Year Olds*. London: HMSO.

Ball, S. (1992) The worst of three worlds: politics, power and teachers. Paper presented to the BEMAS Research Conference, Nottingham, April.

Bagley, C. (1975) The background of deviance: black children in London. In Verma, G. K. and Bagley, C. (eds) *Race and Education across Cultures*. London: Heinemann.

Bagley, C., Mallick, K. and Verma , G (1979) Pupils' self-esteem: a study of black and white teenagers in British schools. In Verma , G. K. and Bagley, C. (eds) *Race, Education and Identity*. London: Macmillan.

Benn, C., Parris, J., Riley, K. A. and Weiner, G. (1982) Education and women: the new agenda. *Socialism and Education* **9**(2), 10–13.

Blackstone, T. and Weinreich-Haste, H. (1980) The right school for girls. *New Society*, 17 February.

Bogart, K. and Stein, N. (1987/89) Breaking the silence: sexual harassment in education. *Peabody Journal of Education* **64**(4), Summer, 146–63.

Bolton, E. (1979) Education in a multiracial society. *Trends in Education* **4**, Winter, 3–7.

Bolton, E. (1992) Imaginary gardens with real toads. Speech to Conference of Local Education Authorities, Liverpool, July.

Bone, A. (1983) *Girls and Girl Only Schools: A Review of the Evidence.* Manchester: Equal Opportunities Commission.

Brehoney, K. (1984) Coeducation: perspectives and debates in the early twentieth century. In Deem, R. (ed.) *Coeducation Reconsidered.* Milton Keynes: Open University Press.

Brown, P. (1990) The third wave: education and the ideology of parentocracy. *British Journal of Sociology of Education* **11**(1), 65–85.

Brown, S. and Riddell, S. (eds) (1992) *Class, Race and Gender in Schools: A New Agenda for Policy and Practice in Scottish Education.* Edinburgh: Scottish Council for Research in Education.

Bull, D. (1980) The anti-discretion movement in Britain: fact or phantom? *Journal of Social Welfare Law.*

Bullock, A., Thomas, H. and Arnott, M. (1993) The impact of local management on schools: a view from head teachers. In Riley, K. A. (ed.) *Local Government Policy-Making* **19**(5), May (special edition on education).

Butler, R. A. (1973) The politics of the 1944 Education Act. In Fowler, G., Morris, V. and Ozga, J. (eds) *Decision-Making in British Education.* London: Heinemann in association with the Open University Press.

Carby, H. V. (1982) White women listen! Black feminism and the boundaries of sisterhood. In Centre for Cultural Studies (ed.) *The Empire Strikes Back: Race and Racism in 70s Britain.* London: Hutchinson.

Carrington, B. (1981) Schooling an underclass: the implications of ethnic differences in attainment, *Durham and Newcastle Research Review* **9**(47), 293–305.

Carter, N. (1989) Performance indicators: backseat drivers or hands-off control? *Policy and Politics* **17**(2), 131–8.

Carter, N. (1991) Learning to measure performance: the use of indicators in organizations. *Public Administration* **69**, Spring, 85–101.

Cave, E. and Wilkinson, C. (1991) Managerial capability: what headteachers need to be good at. In Ribbins, C., Glatter, R., Simkins, T. and Watson, L. (eds) *Developing Educational Leadership.* Harlow: Longman in association with BEMAS.

Chapman, J. (1991) The effectiveness of schooling and of educational resource management: a preliminary analysis of developments in OECD countries. (Unpublished; OECD).

Cicourel, A. V. and Kitsuse, J. I. (1963) *The Educational Decision-Makers.* Indianapolis: Bobs-Merrill.

Clarricoates, K. (1980) The importance of being Ernest . . . Emma . . . Tom . . . Jane, the perception and categorisation of gender conformity and gender deviation in primary schooling. In Deem, R. (ed.) *Schooling for Women's Work.* London: Routledge & Kegan Paul.

Coard, B. (1971) *How the West Indian Child Is Made Educationally Subnormal in the British School System*. London: New Beacon Books for the Caribbean Education and Community Workers' Association, London.

Coleman, J. S., Campbell, E. A., Hobson, C. J., McPartland, J., Mood, A. M., Weinfeld, F. D. and York, R. L. (1966) *Equality of Educational Opportunity*. Washington, DC: US Government Printing Office.

Coleman, P. and Larocque, L. (1990) *Struggling to Be Good Enough: Administrative Practices and School District Ethos*. Lewes: Falmer Press.

Cordingley, P. (1992) The local governance of education. In *Education: A Major Local Authority Service*. Luton: Local Government Management Board.

Cordingley, P. and Kogan, M. (1993) *In Support of Education: The Functioning of Local Government*. London: Jessica Kingsley.

Crowther Report (1959) *Report of the Central Advisory Council for Education, 15–18*. London: HMSO.

Dale, R. R. (1969) *Mixed or Single-Sex School*, Vol. 3. London: Routledge & Kegan Paul.

David, M. E. (1980) *The State, the Family and Education*. London: Routledge & Kegan Paul.

Davies, J. (1981) *Perspectives on Attendance*. London: ILEA Research and Statistics (RS 749/80).

Davies, L. (1990) Women and educational management in the Third World. Paper presented to the conference on Equal Advances in Education Management, Vienna, 3–6 December.

Davis, K. C. (1969) *Discretionary Justice*. Baton Rouge: Louisiana State University Press.

Department of Education and Science (DES) (1971) *The Education of Immigrants* Survey 13. London: HMSO.

DES (1975) *Curricular Differences for Boys and Girls*, Survey 21. London: HMSO.

DES (1977) *Education in Schools: A Consultative Document*, Cmnd 6869. London: HMSO.

Department for Education (DFE) (1992) *The Preparation of Girls for Adult and Working Life (October 1990–July 1991)*, a report by HMI (209/92/NS). London: DFE.

De Lyon, H. (1989) Sexual harassment. In De Lyon, H. and Widdowson Migniuolo, F. (eds) *Women Teachers: Issues and Experiences*. Milton Keynes: Open University Press.

De Lyon, H. and Widdowson Migniuolo, F. (1989) *Women Teachers: Issues and Experiences*. Milton Keynes: Open University Press.

Dicketts, S. and Limb, A. (1991) Total equality management: Milton Keynes College, a case study. In Riley, K. A. (ed.) *Local Government Policy-Making* **18**(1), July.

Driver, G. (1977) Ethnicity, cultural competence and school achievement: a case study of West Indian pupils attending a British secondary modern. PhD thesis, University of Illinois at Urbana.

Driver, G. (1978) *Sex Differences in Secondary School Performance: A Survey of West Indian Minority and English Majority School-Leavers from Five Schools in the North, Midlands and South of England*. London: Commission for Racial Equality.

Driver, G. (1979) Classroom stress and school achievement: West Indian adolescents and their teachers. In Khan, V. (ed.) *Minority Families in Britain*. London: Macmillan.

Driver, G. (1980) How West Indians do better at school (especially the girls). *New Society*, 17 January.

Dyhouse, C. (1981) *Girls Growing Up in Late Victorian and Edwardian England*. London: Routledge & Kegan Paul.

Education Counts: An Indicators Systems to Monitor the Nation's Educational Health (1991). Washington, DC: Special Study Panel on Education Indicators for the National Center for Education Statistics.

Eide, K. (1978) Some key problems of equality in education. Paper for IIEP/Inter-Agency Seminar of Educational Development, 27–30 November.

Equal Opportunities Commission (1991) *Women and Men in Britain in 1991*. Manchester: EOC.

Essen, J. and Ghodsian, M. (1979) The children of immigrants: school performance. *New Community* **7**(3), 422–4.

Floud, J. (1961) Reserve of ability. *Forum* **3**(2), 66–8.

Floud, J. E., Halsey, A. and Martin, F. M. (1956) *Social Class and Educational Opportunity*. London: Heinemann.

Fobbs, J. (1990) Enhancing organizational vision through the perceptions of managerial styles of women Presidents of two-year colleges. Paper presented to the conference on Equal Advances in Education Management, Vienna, 3–6 December.

Foner, N. (1978) *Jamaica Farewell*. London: Routledge & Kegan Paul.

Fuller, M. (1980) Black girls in a London comprehensive. In Deem, R. (ed.) *Schooling for Women's Work*. London: Routledge & Kegan Paul.

Garrison, L. (1979) *Black Youth and Rastafarianism, and the Identity Crisis in Britain*. London: ACER Project Publication.

Gerver, E. and Hart, L. (1990) Surviving in a cold climate: women and decision-making in Scottish Education. Paper presented to the conference on Equal Advances in Education Management, Vienna, 3–6 December.

Giles, R. (1977) *The West Indian Experience in British Schools: Multiracial Education and Social Disadvantage in London*. London: Heinemann.

Gilmartin, K. J. (1980) *The Status of Women and Minorities in Education: A Social Indicator Feasibility Study*. Washington, DC: National Center for Education Statistics.

Gipps, C. (1990) The social implications of national assessment. Paper presented to the annual conference of the British Sociological Association, London, 2–5 April.

Goodlad, J. I. (1984) *A Place Called School: Prospects for the Future*. New York: McGraw-Hill.

Hafner, A. L. and Shaha, S. (1984) Gender differences in the prediction of freshmen grades. Paper presented to the Annual Meeting of the American Educational Research Association, New Orleans, April.

Hansard Society (1990) *Report of the Hansard Society Commission on Women at the Top*. London: Hansard Society.

Helgesen, S. (1990) *The Female Advantage: Women's Ways of Leadership.* New York: Doubleday/Currency.

Henkel, M. (1991) *Government, Evaluation and Change.* London: Jessica Kingsley.

HMSO (1992) *Choice and Diversity: A New Framework for Schools.* Cmnd 2021. London: HMSO.

House of Commons (1973) *Education*, Vol. 1 of Report no. 405 of the Select Committee on Race Relations and Immigration. London: HMSO.

House of Commons (1980–81) *Fifth Reading of the Home Affairs Committee, Racial Disadvantage.* London: HMSO.

House of Commons (1987) *Order for the Second Reading of the Education Reform Bill*, 1 December. London: HMSO.

Hutchinson, G. (1993) To go boldly, shaping the future without the LEA. In Riley, K. A. (ed.) *Local Government Policy-Making*, **19**(5), May (a special edition on education).

Inner London Education Authority (ILEA) (1982) *Sex Differences and Achievement* (RS/823/82). London: ILEA.

ILEA (1984) *Improving Secondary Schools: Report of the Committee on the Curriculum and Organization of Secondary Schools*, chaired by D. H. Hargreaves. London: ILEA.

ILEA (1987) *Analysis of Fifth Year Examination Results.* London: ILEA.

ILEA (1988) *Suspensions and Expulsions from School, 1987/88.* London: ILEA.

Kant, L. (1987) National curriculum: notionally equal. *National Union of Teachers, Education Review*, Autumn, 41–4.

Kaufman, D. and Fetters, M. (1980) Work motivation and values among professional men and women: a new accounting. *Journal of Vocational Behaviour* **17**, 251–62.

Kleinwort Benson Securities (1991) *Economic Comment: The Economic Cost of Being Bottom of the Class*, August. London: Kleinwort Benson.

Lavigueur, J. (1980) Coeducation and the tradition of separate needs. In Spender, D. and Sarah, E. (eds) *Learning to Lose: Sexism and Education.* London: The Women's Press.

Leavitt, H. J. and Lipman-Blumen, J. (1980) A case for the relational manager. *Organizational Dynamics*, Summer.

Leithwood, K., Jantzi, D. and Dart, B. (1991) Towards a multi-level conception of policy implementation processes based on commitment strategies. Paper presented to the International Congress on School Effectiveness, Cardiff.

Leithwood, K., Steinbach, R. and Begley, P. (1991) The nature and contribution of socialization experiences to becoming a principal in Canada. Paper presented to the International Congress on School Effectiveness, Cardiff.

Lidstrom, A. (1991) *Discretion: An Art of the Possible*, Research Report 1991:5. Department of Political Science, University of Umea, Sweden.

Little, A., Mabey, C. and Whitaker, G. (1968) The education of immigrant children in Inner London primary schools. *Race*, **9**(4), April.

Local Government Information Unit (1991a) *Priority for Equality.* London: LGIU.

Local Government Information Unit (1991b) *New Directions in Local Government: Quality and Equality.* London: LGIU.

Local Government Management Board (1991) *Equality and Quality: Services to the Whole Community.* Luton: LGMB.

Lord, J. (1992) New directions for schools and colleges. In *A Focus on Education as a Major Local Authority Service.* Luton: Local Government Management Board.

Lundgren, U. P. (1986) *Att Organisera Skolan.* Stockholm: Liber.

Mabey, C. (1980) *Black British Literacy: A Study of Reading Attainment of London Black Children from 8–15 Years.* London: ILEA.

Mac an Ghaill, M. (1988) *Young, Gifted and Black: Student Teacher Relations in the Schooling of Black Youth.* Milton Keynes: Open University Press.

MacDonald, B., Bhavani, R., Khan, L. and John, G. (1989) *Murder in the Playground: The Report of the MacDonald Inquiry into Racism and Racial Violence in Manchester Schools* (The Burnage Report). Manchester: Longsight Press.

Macdonald, J. and Piggott, J. (1990) *Global Quality: The New Management Culture.* London: Mercury Books.

McGregor Burns, J. (1978) *Leadership.* New York: Harper & Row.

McPherson, A. and Raab, C. (1988) *Governing Education: A Sociology of Policy since 1945.* Edinburgh: Edinburgh University Press.

McRobbie, A. (1978) Working-class girls and the culture of feminity. In *Women Take Issue.* London: Hutchinson.

Manley-Casimir, M. (1991) Taking the road not taken: reframing education administration for another day – a critique and proposal. In Ribbins, P., Glatter, R., Simkins, T. and Watson, L. (eds) *Developing Education Leaders.* Harlow: Longman in association with BEMAS.

Mays, A. M. M. (1990) *The AHEAD Program.* Paper presented to the conference on Equal Advances in Education Management, Vienna, 3–6 December.

Migniuolo, F. and De Lyon, H. (eds) (1989) *Women Teachers: Issues and Experiences.* Milton Keynes: Open University Press.

Miles, S. and Middleton, C. (1990) Girls' education in the balance: the ERA and inequality. In Flude, M. and Hammer, M. (eds) *The Education Reform Act 1988: Its Origins and Implications.* London: Falmer Press.

National Center for Educational Statistics (1984) Science and mathematics education in American high schools: results from the High School and Beyond study. *Bulletin of the US Department of Education.* Washington, DC: US Government Printing Office.

National Curriculum Council (1990) *Education for Industrial Understanding,* Curriculum Guidance 4. York: NCC.

National Union of Teachers (1990) *Promotion and the Woman Teacher – Ten Years On.* London: NUT.

Nava, M. (1984) The urban, the domestic and education for girls. In Grace, G. (ed.) *Education and the City: Theory, History and Contemporary Practice.* London: Routledge & Kegan Paul.

Netherlands Centre for School Improvement (1990) Step by step to affirmative action. Paper presented to the conference on Equal Advances in Education Management, Vienna, 3–6 December.

Norwood Report (1943) *Curriculum and Examinations in Secondary Schools*, Secondary Schools Examination Council. London: HMSO.

Nylen, C. and Sorhuus, E. (1990) In search of equality. Paper presented to the conference on Equal Advances in Education Management, Vienna, 3–6 December.

Oakes, J. (1989) What educational indicators? The case for assessing the school context. *Educational Evaluation and Policy Analysis* **11**(2), 181–99.

OECD (1985/86) Women in educational management. Statistical update to the conference on Equal Advances in Education Management, Vienna, 3–6 December. Paris: OECD.

OECD (1989) *Schools and Quality: An International Report.* Paris: OECD.

OECD (1992) *Education at a Glance.* Paris: OECD.

Ouston, J., Gold, A. and Gosling, P. (1992) Development of managers in education: do men and women differ? Paper presented to BEMAS Research Conference, Nottingham.

Page, R. and Nash, M. (1980) Teenage attitudes to technology and industry. Mimeograph produced for the Standing Conference on Schools' Science and Technology, June.

Pedley, R. (1963) *The Comprehensive School.* London: Penguin.

Penn, H. and Riley, K. A. (1992) *Managing Services for the Under-Fives.* Harlow: Longman.

Peters, T. and Waterman, R. (1982) *In Search of Excellence.* New York: Harper & Row.

Pettersen, K. (1990) Women and educational leadership in Norway. Paper presented to the conference on Equal Advances in Education Management, Vienna, 3–6 December.

Pound, R. (1960) Discretion, dispensation and mitigation: the problem of the individual special case. *NYUL Review* **35**, 926.

Purvis, J. (1984) *Gender, Race and Education* (Open University E205). Milton Keynes: Open University Press.

Rampton, A. (Chairman) (1981) *West Indian Children in Our Schools: Interim Report of the Committee of Inquiry into the Education of Children from Ethnic Minority Groups.* London: HMSO.

Ranfil-Guggenberger, D. (1990) Women in school management. Paper presented to the conference on Equal Advances in Education Management, Vienna, 3–6 December.

Ranger, C. (1988) *Ethnic Minority School Teachers.* London: Commission for Racial Equality.

Ranson, S. and Thomas, H. (1989) Education reform: consumer democracy, or social democracy? In Stewart, J. and Stoker, G. (eds) *The Future of Local Government.* Basingstoke: Macmillan Education.

Reid, E. (1989) Black girls talking. In Foster-Carter, O. and Wright, C. (eds) *Gender and Education* **1**(3) (special issue on race).

Rex, J. and Tomlinson, S. (1979) *Colonial Immigrants in a British City.* London: Routledge & Kegan Paul.

Ribbins, P., Glatter, R., Simkins, T. and Watson, L. (eds) (1991) *Developing Educational Leaders.* Harlow: Longman in association with BEMAS.

Riddell, S. (1992) Gender and education: progressive and conservative forces in the balance. In Brown, S. and Riddell, S. (eds) *Class, Race and Gender in Schools: A New Agenda for Policy and Practice in Scottish Education.* Edinburgh: Scottish Council for Research in Education.

Riley, K. A. (1982) Policing the police, teaching the teachers: Scarman, Rampton and MPs read the riot lessons. *Multiracial Education* **10**(2), 63–76.

Riley, K. A. (1985a) Attitudes and aspirations of girls of Afro-Caribbean origin. PhD dissertation, Bulmershe College of Higher Education, University of London and Department of Education, Cambridge University.

Riley, K. A. (1985b) Black girls speak for themselves. In Weiner, G. (ed.) *Just a Bunch of Girls.* Milton Keynes: Open University Press.

Riley, K. A. (1990a) Equality for women – the role of local authorities. In *Local Government Studies*, Jan/Feb, 49–68.

Riley, K. A. (1990b) Making indicators consumer friendly. *Education* **11**, 470–72.

Riley, K. A. (1992a) *Education Indicators and the Search for Quality.* Luton: Local Government Management Board.

Riley, K. A. (1992b) The changing framework and purposes of education authorities. In *Research Papers in Education, Policy and Practice* **7**(1), 3–25.

Riley, K. A. (1992c) Following the education indicators trail in the pursuit of quality. Paper presented to International Congress for School Effectiveness and Improvement, Victoria, British Columbia, January.

Riley, K. A. and Nuttall, D. L. (1994) *Education Indicators: UK and International Perspectives.* Lewes: Falmer Press.

Rogers, A. and Gilligan, C. (1988) *Translating Girls' Voices: Two Languages of Development*, Cambridge, Mass.: Harvard University Graduate School of Education.

Rubinstein, D. and Simon, B. (1969) *The Evolution of the Comprehensive School, 1926–1972.* London: Routledge & Kegan Paul.

Ruby, A., Millan, M. and Howe, V. (1989) Indicators for equity: a neglected part of the debate. Paper presented to the Australian Conference of Directors-General of Education, Sydney, July.

Rutter, M., Maughan, B., Mortimore, P., Ouston, J. with Smith, A. (1979) *Fifteen Thousand Hours: Secondary Schools and Their Effects on Children.* London: Open Books; Cambridge, Mass.: Harvard University Press.

Rosener, J. B. (1990) Ways women lead. *Harvard Business Review.* Nov/Dec.

Safia Mirza, H. (1992) *Young, Female and Black.* London and New York: Routledge.

Scarman (1981) *The Brixton Disorders: 10th April–12th April 1981.* Cmnd 8427. London: HMSO.

Schuijt, L. (1990) Women in middle management: an in-between step to leadership. Paper presented to the conference on Equal Advances in Education Management, Vienna, 3–6 December.

Shakeshaft, C. (1990) Gender and supervision. Paper presented to the conference on Equal Advances in Education Management, Vienna, 3–6 December.

Shakeshaft, C. and Cohan, A. (1990) In loco parentis: Sexual abuse of students in school. Paper presented to the American Educational Research Association, Annual Meeting, Boston, March.

Shakeshaft, C. (1992) Gender issues and the implementation of effective policies and practices in schools. Paper presented to the International Congress for School Effectiveness and Improvement, Victoria, British Columbia, January.

Shaw, J. (1980) Education and the individual: schooling for girls or mixed schooling – a mixed blessing? In Deem, R. (ed.) *Schooling for Women's Work*. London: Routledge & Kegan Paul.

Shaw, J. (1984) The politics of single-sex schools. In Deem, R. (ed.) *Coeducation Reconsidered*. Milton Keynes: Open University Press.

Silver, P. and Silver, H. (1974) *The Education of the Poor*. London: Routledge & Kegan Paul.

Skelcher, C. (1992) Improving the quality of local public services. *Service Industries Journal*, **12**(4), 463–77.

Spender, D. and Sarah, E. (eds) (1980) *Learning to Lose: Sexism and Education*. London: The Women's Press.

Stewart, J. and Walsh, K. (1990) *In Search of Quality*. Luton: Local Government Management Board.

Stobart, G., Elwood, J. and Quinlan, M. (1992) Gender bias in examinations: how equal are the opportunities? *British Educational Research Journal* **18**(3), 261–76.

Taylor, M. J. (1981) *Caught Between: A Review of Research into the Education of Pupils of West Indian Origin*. Slough: NFER/Nelson.

Taylor, M. J. (1992) *Equality after ERA? Concerns and Challenges for Multicultural and Antiracist Education*. Slough: NFER.

Tobin, K. and Garnett, P. (1987) Gender related differences in science activities. *Science Education* **71**, 91–103.

Tomlinson, S. (1980) The educational performance of ethnic minority children. *New Community*, **8**(3), 213–34.

Townsend, E. M. and Brittan, E. M. (1972) *Organization in Multiracial Schools*. Slough: NFER.

Townsend, H. E. R. (1971) *Immigrant Pupils in England: The LEA Response*. Slough: NFER.

Troyna, B. (1978) Race streaming, a case study. *Educational Review* **30**(1), 59–65.

US Department of Education (1983) *A Nation at Risk*. Report of the National Commission on Excellence in Education. Washington, DC: Department of Education.

Vernon, P. E. (ed.) (1957) *Secondary School Selection*. London: Methuen.

Walden, R. and Walkerdine, V. (1985) *Girls and Mathematics: From Primary to Secondary School*. Bedford Way Papers 24. London: University of London, Institute of Education.

Walsh, K. (1992) Rights, contracts and charters. In *Education: A Major Local Authority Service*. Luton: Local Government Management Board.

Willetts, D. (1992) *Modern Conservatism*. Harmondsworth: Penguin.

Willms, J. D. and Kerr, P. (1988) Changes in sex differences in Scottish examination results since 1976. *Journal of Early Adolescence* **7**, 85–105.

Young, K. and Spencer, L. (1990) *Women Managers in Local Government: Removing the Barriers.* Luton: Local Government Management Board.

Name index

Note: Page references in **bold** type refer to **figures**. Page references in *italic* type refer to *tables*.

Addison, B. 104
Alban Metcalfe, B. N. 92
Al-Khalifa, E. 91, 103, 104
Anthias, F. 55
Arnot, M. 12, 21, 24, 27

Bagley, C. 52, 71, 83-4
Baker, K. 17, 19, 31
Ball, S. 20
Beale, Miss D. 89, 93
Begley, P. 90
Benn, C. 23
Blackstone, T. 39
Bogart, K. 47
Bolton, E. 20, 47, 49
Bone, A. 39
Brehoney, K. 38–9
Brittan, E. M. 48, 49
Brown, P. 21
Brown, S. 31
Bull, D. 10
Bullock, A. 27
Buss, Miss F. M. 89, 93
Butler, R. A. 17

Callaghan, James 19
Carby, H. V. 84
Carrington, B. 56
Carter, N. 110, 114, 114–15
Cave, E. 103
Chapman, J. 9
Cicourel, A. V. 60
Clarricoates, K. 40
Coard, B. 48
Cohan, A. 108
Coleman, J. S. 119
Coleman, P. 126
Cordingley, P. 21, 30

Dale, R. R. 38
Dart, B. 97–100, *99*, **102**, 102
David, M. E. 36
Davies, J. 51–2
Davies, L. 88, 89, 90, 92
Davis, K. C. 10, **14**
De Lyon, H. 26, 90, 97, 108, 109
Dicketts, S. *133*
Driver, G. 49–50, 52, 56, 69
Dyhouse, C. 55

Eide, K. 15
Elwood, J. 44
Essen, J. 50

Fetters, M. 92
Floud, J. E. 17, 36, 55
Fobbs, J. 101, **102**, 102
Foner, N. 52, 55, 71
Fuller, M. 52

Garnett, P. 46
Garrison, L. 55
Gerver, E. 88, 93, 96, 102
Ghodsian, M. 50
Giles, R. 50
Gilligan, C. 46
Gilmartin, K. J. 117–18
Gipps, C. 24
Glatter, R. 104
Gold, A. 90, 132
Goodlad, J. I. 119
Gosling, P. 90, 132

Hafner, A. L. 44
Halsey, A. 55
Hart, L. 88, 93, 96, 102
Helgesen, S. 96–7
Henkel, M. 109
Howe, V. 107, 115
Hutchinson, G. 134

Jantzi, D. 97–100, *99*, **102**, 102

Kant, L. 24
Kaufman, D. 92
Kerr, P. 44
Kitsuse, J. I. 60
Kogan, M. 30

Lamb, A. *132*
Larocque, L. 126
Lavigueur, J. 89
Lawlor, S. 43
Leavitt, H. J. 101
Leithwood, K. 90, 97–100, *99*, **102**, 102
Lidstrom, A. 10
Limb, A. *133*
Lipman–Blumen, J. 101
Little, A. 48
Lord, J. 30
Lundgren, U. P. 90

Mabey, C. 48, 50
Mac an Ghaill, M. 52
MacDonald, B. 55
Macdonald, J. 4
McGregor Burns, J. 95
McPherson, A. 55
McRobbie, A. 41, 44
Mallick, K. 52, 71
Manley-Casimir, M. 10–11
Martin, F. M. 55
Maughan, B. 39, 53
Mays, A. M. M. 134
Middleton, C. 24, 107
Migniuolo, F. 90, 109
Miles, S. 24, 107
Millan, M. 107, 115
Mortimore, P. 39, 53

Nash, M. 40
Nava, M. 35, 36
Nicholson, N. 92, *93*
Nuttall, D. L 110, 114
Nylen, C. 130

Oakes, J. 118–20
Ouston, J. 39, 53, 90, 132

Page, R. 40
Pedley, R. 37
Penn, H. 126
Peters, T. 4
Pettersen, K. 130
Piggott, J. 4
Pound, R. 10
Purvis, J. 36

Quinlan, M. 44

Raab, C. 55
Ranfil-Guggenberger, D. 92
Ranger, C. 89
Ranson, S. 18
Reid, E. 52
Rex, J. 49
Ribbins, P. 104
Riddell, S. 24, 25, 31, 44, 45, 82
Riley, K. A. 5, 11, 12, 13, 31, 49, 52, 53, 57, *58*, *73*, 96, 108, 110, 114, 115, 123–4, 126
Rogers, A. 46
Rosener, J. B. 95–6, 99, **102**, 102
Rubinstein, D. 18, 31, 36–7
Ruby, A. 107, 115
Rutter, M. 39, 53

Safia Mirza, H. 55, 72, 74
Sarah, E. 40
Schuijt, L. 132
Shaha, S. 44
Shakeshaft, C. 47, 90, 100–1, **102**, 102, 103, 108
Shaw, J. 38, 39
Silver, H. 35

Silver, P. 35
Simkins, T. 104
Simon, B. 18, 31, 36–7
Skelcher, C. 5–6, *6*
Smith, A. 39, 53
Sorhuus, E. 130
Spencer, L. 97
Spender, D. 40
Stein, N. 47
Steinbach, R. 90
Stewart, J. 6–7
Stewart, M. 18
Stobart, G. 44

Taylor, M. J. 25–6, 27, 48, 51, 55
Thatcher, Margaret 18
Thomas, H. 18, 27
Tobin, K. 46
Tomlinson, S. 49, 50
Townsend, E. M. 48, 49
Townsend, H. E. R. 48
Troyna, B. 49

Verma, G. 52, 71
Vernon, P. E. 17

Walden, R. 24
Walkerdine, V. 24
Walsh, K. 6–7, 21
Waterman, R. 4
Watson, L. 104
Weiner, G. (Benn *et al.*) 23
Weinrich-Haste, H. 39
Whitaker, G. 48
White, J. 96, 104
Widdowson Migniuolo, F. 26, 91
Wilkinson, C. 103
Willetts, D. 127–8
Willms, J. D. 44

Young, K. 97
Yuval Davis, N. 55

Subject Index

Note: Page references in **bold** type refer to **figures**. Page references in *italic* type refer to *tables*.

absence rate 51–2
accountability 5, *6*, 18, 19, 21, 122–3, 126
Afro-Caribbean children, *see* West Indian children
AHEAD course (Canada) 134
ambition 92
American Association of University Women (AAUW) 45–6
anti-Conservative concept 127
Asian children 51, 52
Association of University Teachers (AUT) 89
attainment 20
  see also National Curriculum
Audit Commission 109, 110–11, 123
Australia, state of Victoria 27, 91
Austria 91–2

Birmingham, *see under* sexual harassment
black children 47–9, 50–1, 55, 70, 71–2
  boys' behaviour 50, 69–70
  colour–blind stance 49–50, 68, 74, 75
  girls 52, 53, 57–84, 74
  see also West Indian children
boys 43–4, 50, 69–70
Brixton Riots (1981) 53–4

Camden Girls' School 89
Canada 97–100, 134
careers 60, 80, 82
CBI (Confederation for British Industry) 16, 129
Cheltenham Ladies' College 89
Christchurch School 62–4, 70
  gender issues 62–4, *73*, 73, 74
  race issues 66–9, 74, 75
city technology colleges 19, 28, 130
class 37–8, 59, 70–2, 127
  and gender 35–7, 55, 70, 74–5
  and race 55, 74–5
coeducation 37, 38–9, 40
coeducational schools 41, 43
  see also Greenvale School; Marchbank School
'colour–blind' approach 49–50, 68, 74, 75
Commission for Racial Equality (CRE) 88–9, 104
comprehensive education 17–18, 23, 37, 38, 127
comprehensive schools, *see* Crossland School; Greenvale School
Crossland School 70
  gender and race issues 62–4, *73*, 73, 74, 75
Crowther Report (1959) 36–7, 70
cultural pluralism 49
curriculum 23–4, 35–6, 40, 62–4, 70
  'choice mechanism' 60–2
  overt 23, 64
  see also hidden curriculum; National Curriculum
'customer', of education 4–5, 8, **9**, 19, 127; *see also* market mechanisms
customer care initiatives 6–7, 8

data collection 124, **125**
database 28, 109–11, 126
Denmark 88
Department for Education (DFE) 41–4, 88, 125
Department of Education and Science (DES) 39–40, 48
Disabled Persons Employment Act (1944) 9
discretion 9, 10–12, 13, **14**, 128–9
  of LEAs 130–1
discrimination 12–13, 26–7, 44, 50–1
domestic roles 35–6, 40–1, 70, 81–2
domestic subjects 36

Education 26–7
Education Acts
  (1944) 17–18, 26, 31, 36, 127
  (1993) 26–7, 29–30
  Reform Act (1988) 17, 19–20, *22*, 25–6, 31, 55, 127
education (performance) indicators 109–26, **125**
educational outcomes 13, 109
educational process 108–9
educationally subnormal schools, *see* ESN schools
egalitarian policies 127–8
'11 plus' 17
employment opportunities 106, 129
environment, educational 108–9
Equal Opportunities Commission (EOC) 90–1
Equal Pay Act (1970) 40
  amendment (1983) 10, 91
equality
  of opportunity 9, 12, 13, 15
    and Education Reform Act (1988) *22*
    and National Curriculum *22*, 23–5
  of outcome 13
  programmes 12–13
ESN schools 48, 50, 51
ethnic minorities *58*, 58, 106, *113*, 113
  educational performance 50–1, 115–16, *116*
  as teachers 88–9
  see also Asian children; black children; West Indian children
European Community (EC) 110
Evening Standard 116–17
examination performance, *see* performance, examination

feminism 82
Fifteen Thousand Hours (Rutter) 53
Financial Times 29
funding 28–9, 130
Funding Agency for Schools (FAS) 29
Funding Council for Further Education (FEFC) 20
further education 20, 111

gender 39–40, 59–64, *113*, 113, 127
  balance in teaching 88

Christchurch 62–4, *73*, 73, 74
  and class 35–7, 55, 74–5
  in comprehensive education 38
  Crossland 62–4, 74, 75
  disadvantage 37–8
  and educational outcomes 109
  equality 23–5
  and examination performance *73*, 73, 115–16,
    116
  Greenvale 59–62, 69–70, 74, 75
  impact in schools 43–4
  inequality 41–5, 45–7, 129
  and management and leadership 99–100
  Marchbank 76–9, 82
  and race 55, 69–70, 74–5
gender-blind approach 59–60
girls 35–7, 40, 70–1, 72, 82
  adulthood preparation 41–5
  black 52, 53, 74
    and white 57–84
  disadvantage challenge 44
  examination performance *73*, 73, 115–16, *116*
governing bodies 29, 132
grammar schools 36, 37
  see also Christchurch School
grant-maintained schools 19, 20, *22*, 28–9, 30, 130
Green Paper on Education (1977) 49
Greenvale School
  gender issues 59–62, 69–70, *73*, 73, 74, 75
  race issues 64–6, 69–70, 74
Greenwich judgment 28, 31
Guardian, The 13, 29

Hargreaves Report (1984) 37–8
headship appointments 26–7
hidden curriculum 23, 40–1, 59–62, 76, 108
higher education 89
Hillingdon 28
hiring practices 100–1, 132
HMI (Her Majesty's Inspectorate) 39–40, 41–4,
  111

ILEA (Inner London Education Authority) 28, 39,
  48, 83–4
  examination performance *83*, *116*, 116
  Research and Statistics Department 50, *83*
  suspensions *112*, 112–14, *113*
incentive allowances 91, 107
Independent on Sunday, The 16
indicators
  education, *see* education (performance)
    indicators
  of quality 133–4
industrial tribunals 91
inspection 5, 19

Japan 4

Kleinwort Benson Securities 20

labour market 80–1, 82
leadership 87–104, 129, 130
  national management initiatives 103–4
  styles 93–100, **94**, **102**, 102, 104
  and women **94**, 97, **102**, 102, 131–2, 134
  see also discretion
league tables 105, 129
learning process 119–20
life choices 92–3, *93*

local education authorities (LEAs) 5–6, 27–8,
  30–1, 128
  discretion of 11, 130–1
  use of education indicators 122–6, **125**
local government 6, 13, 130–1
local management of schools (LMS) *22*, 26–7
loyalty 100

male domination 59–62, 75, 76, 82, 101, 108
management, *see* leadership
Management Charter Initiative (MCI) 103
Marchbank School 57, 75–83, 133
  gender issues 76–9, 82
  race issues 79–80
market mechanisms 19, 20–1, 28, 87, 106
measuring 106–9
meritocracy 127–8
middle class 35–7, 70
middle management 132
Milton Keynes College 132, *133*
MORI, pupil exclusions study (1993) 31

National Child Development Study 50
National Curriculum 19, 20, *22*, 23–6, 122
  Standard Assessment Tasks (SATs) 24, 105
National Curriculum Council 25
national government 9, 121–2, 129–30
National Union of Teachers (NUT) 97, 104, 108
  teacher pay survey (1990) 91, 107
Netherlands 88, 129, 130
Netherlands Centre for School Improvement 130
North London Collegiate 36, 89
Northern Ireland 10
Norway 129, 130
Norwood Report (1943) 36
nursery school 23, 46

Office for Standards in Education (OFSTED) 107,
  111
Opportunity 2000 129
Organisation for Economic Co-operation and
  Development (OECD) 9, 20, 88, 110, 121
  Report (1989) 3, 18
overt curriculum, *see* curriculum

parental concerns 28
Parents' Charter 21
patriarchy 84
pay differentials 90–1, 107
performance
  educational 18, 19, 21, 42, 129
    coeducation/single-sex schooling 38, 39
    of ethnic minorities 50–3, 115–16, *116*
    league tables 105, 129
    see also education (performance) indicators
  examination 44, *83*, 83, 115–16, *116*
    black children 51, 52, 53, 70, 71–2
    girls 72–4, *73*
policies 9–10, 18–19, 129–33
power 13, 19–20, 29
pre-school education 23, 46
primary schools 23, 88
private sector 4–6, *6*
promotion 106, *132*, 132
public sector 4–6, *6*
public spending 13
pupil exclusions, *see* suspensions, pupil

qualitative reflection 124–5, **125**
quality

definitions 3–4, 6, **14**, 15
framework **7**, 7–8

race 59, 106, 127
   Christchurch 66–9, 74, 75
   and class 55, 69–70, 74–5
   Crossland 64–6
   and gender 55, 69–70, 74–5
   Greenvale 64–6, 69–70, 74
   Marchbank 79–80
   and National Curriculum 24, 25–6
Race Relations Act (1975) 9
racism 49–52, 54, 55, 65–9, 75
   Marchbank 79, 81, 82–3
Rampton Report (1981) 51, 53–4
recreational activities 61–2, 77–8, 82
recruitment 100–1, *132*, 132
resources 8–9, **9**, 12–13, 107
responsibility allowances 91, 107
Ruskin Speech (Callaghan 1976) 19

Scarman Report (1981) 53–4
School Management Task Force 103
schools 30, 131, 132
   admissions 28, 31
   subjects 39–40, 42, 59–64
science and technology 23–4, 38, 46
Scotland 44, 45, 93, 96
secondary modern schools 36
secondary schools 23, 88
Select Committee on Race Relations 48
Sex Discrimination Act (1975) 9, 40
sex stereotyping 40–1, 55, 75
sexism 81, 82–3
sexual harassment 46–7, 77, 97, 101, 108
   Birmingham study 97, 104, 108
sexuality 100–1
single-sex schooling 37, 38–9, 40, 42–3
   see also Christchurch School; Crossland School
social justice 8–9, 12, 21
staff, teaching 8, **9**, 26–7, 129, 132

Standard Assessment Tests (SATs), *see* National
   Curriculum
stereotyping 24, 40–1, 75
   black children 50, 55, 69–70
Stratford School 29
suspensions, pupil 29, 31
   see also ILEA
Sweden 129–30

tapestried careers 93
teacher appraisal 103–4
teacher development 26
teacher training 26, 107
Teachers' Pay and Conditions Act (1987) 91, 107
teaching process 119–20
technical schools 31
10/65 Circular 18, 37
'ten-year' rule 47–8
tensions and dilemmas 8, **9**, 28–31
Times Educational Supplement 24, 28, 45
Times, The 17
tripartite system 17, 36, 56

under-achievement, black children 47–8, 49, 51,
   52, 53
USA (United States of America) 4, 44, 45–7, 90
   Education Counts 121–2
   National Center for Educational Statistics 44

West Indian children 48, 49–53, 70–1, 72
white girls 57–84
White Papers
   *Choice and Diversity: A New Framework for
   Schools* (1992) 29
   Framework for Expansion (1972) 18
women 26–7, 42–3, 106
   see also leadership
women's movement 38
woodwork 63
working class 35–7, 40–1, 70